ITALY'S SIBILLINI NATIONAL PARK

by
Gillian Price

2 POLICE SQUARE, MILNTHORPE, CUMBRIA LA7 7PY
www.cicerone.co.uk

First edition 2009
ISBN: 978 185284 535 3
Reprinted 2013 (with updates)

Printed by KHL Printing, Singapore.

A catalogue record for this book is available from the British Library.

Maps and diagrams by Nicola Regine.
Photographs by Gillian Price.

Dedication

For dear Emma *con affetto.*

Advice to Readers

While every effort is made by our authors to ensure the accuracy of guidebooks as they go to print, changes can occur during the lifetime of an edition. If we know of any, there will be an Updates tab on this book's page on the Cicerone website (www.cicerone.co.uk), so please check before planning your trip. We also advise that you check information about such things as transport, accommodation and shops locally. Even rights of way can be altered over time. We are always grateful for information about any discrepancies between a guidebook and the facts on the ground, sent by email to info@cicerone.co.uk or by post to Cicerone, 2 Police Square, Milnthorpe LA7 7PY, United Kingdom.

Front cover: Castelluccio and its famed flowered fields (Walk 19)

CONTENTS

APPENDIX

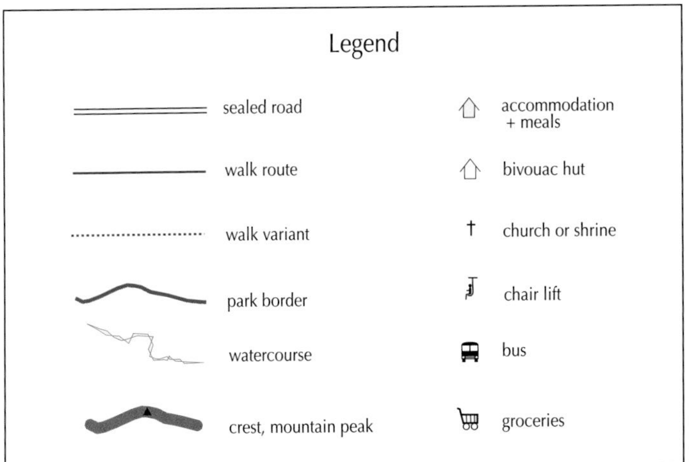
Legend
sealed road
walk route
walk variant
park border
watercourse
crest, mountain peak
accommodation + meals
bivouac hut
church or shrine
chair lift
bus
groceries

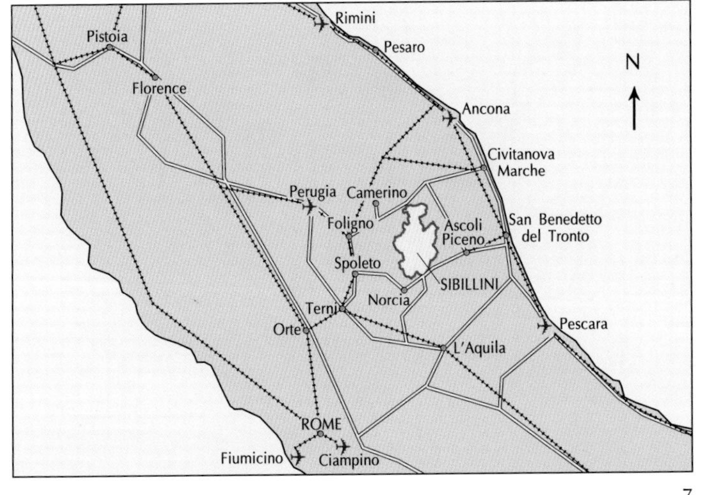
Rimini
Pistoia
Pesaro
Florence
N
Ancona
Civitanova Marche
Perugia
Camerino
Foligno
Ascoli Piceno
San Benedetto del Tronto
Spoleto
SIBILLINI
Norcia
Terni
Orte
Pescara
L'Aquila
ROME
Fiumicino
Ciampino

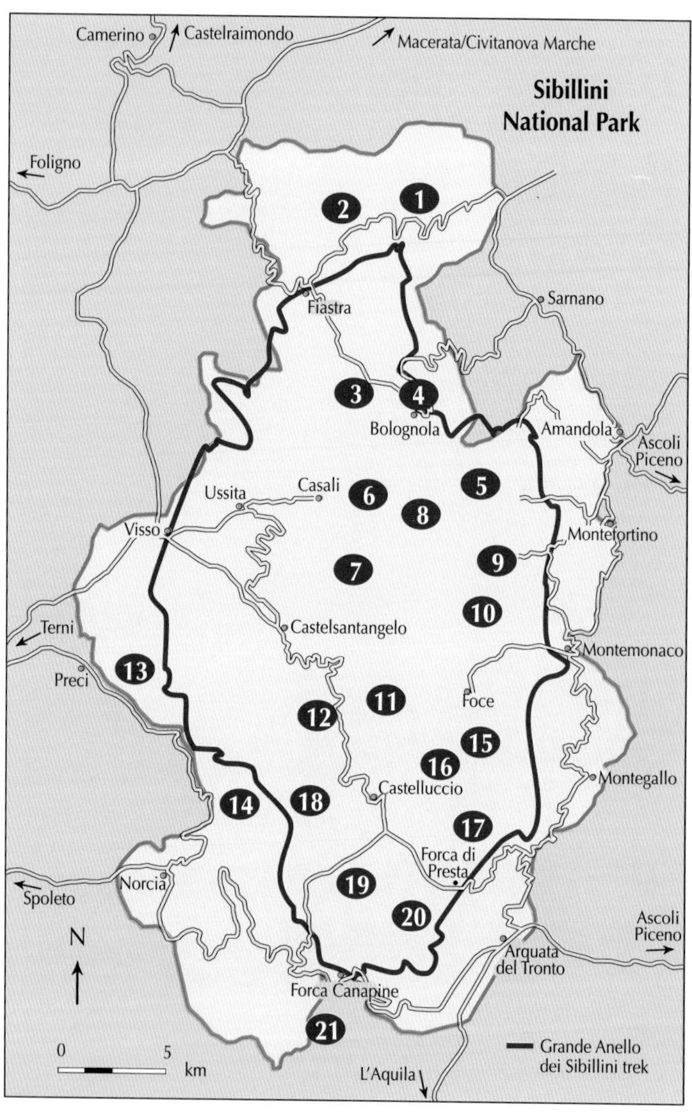
Camerino
Castelraimondo
Macerata/Civitanova Marche
Sibillini National Park
Foligno
1
2
Fiastra
Sarnano
3
4
Bolognola
Amandola
Ascoli Piceno
Casali
Ussita
5
6
8
Visso
Montefortino
9
7
10
Castelsantangelo
Terni
Montemonaco
Preci
13
11
Foce
12
15
16
Montegallo
Castelluccio
14
18
17
Forca di Presta
Norcia
19
Spoleto
20
Ascoli Piceno
N
Arquata del Tronto
Forca Canapine
21
0
5
km
L'Aquila
Grande Anello dei Sibillini trek

INTRODUCTION

MONTI SIBILLINI

Little known to foreign visitors, the Sibillini, in Italy's central Apennine chain, comprise soaring limestone mountains and awe-inspiring natural landscapes inhabited by wonderful wildlife. Rugged lofty ridges link dizzy peaks above vast bare flanks swept by howling winds. Vast grassy uplands are smothered with vivid wildflowers. In dramatic contrast, worlds below, plunging gorges are run through with deliciously cold streams. The thickly wooded valleys are dotted with utterly charming historic villages, home to herders and woodcutters, hard-working reticent folk with a great sense of hospitality. With a good 50 peaks, many over 2000m, there is plenty of exploratory walking to be done in the Sibillini on the intricate web of pathways and old cart tracks. Thanks to dedicated nature lovers and environmental activists, in 1993 this wonderland finally became the Parco Nazionale dei Monti Sibillini, encompassing 700km^2.

Part of Italy's backbone, the Monti Sibillini are a narrow line

Monte Bove Nord, GAS Stage 1

Parco Nazionale dei Monti Sibillini sign

of ridges that act as the watershed between the Adriatic and the Tyrrhenian seas. Straddling the regions of Umbria to the west and Marche to the east they run north–south for almost 40km. Limestone is the main constituent, formed 200 million years ago in a shallow sea and forced skywards. Glaciers later left recognisable traces such as cirques and U-shaped troughs. The stark bareness of these mountains is striking, as few trees exceed the 1500m level.

However, much of this bareness is caused by man as dense forests of beech once cloaked the uplands. These were dramatically cut back over time to create pasture for the armies of sheep – once totalling 400,000 – key to the region's economy.

A number of important rivers run through the range: the Nera has its source in the heart of the Sibillini and flows out through Umbria, whereas the eastern flanks give rise to the Aso, Tenna, Ambro and Fiastrone which head down to the Adriatic coast.

And the name? Sibillini glides over the tongue. In antiquity Sibyls were well known across the Mediterranean as oracles. And one such magnificent prophetess dwelt in a cavern on what is now known as Monte Sibilla, attended by bevies of gorgeous fairy handmaidens. The stuff of fairy tales. Ephemeral beings are hard to avoid in these mountains, as reflected in the place names, an entertaining mix of sacred and profane: Redeemer Peak (Cima del Redentore) and Holy Valley (Valle Santa) vs Devil's Point (Pizzo del Diavolo) and Hell Gorge (Gole dell'Infernaccio)!

WALKING

The wondrously varied landscapes of the Sibillini make for memorable outdoor holidays at any time of year, and holidaymakers of all grades of walking expertise will find something to get their boots into. There are leisurely strolls across flowered meadows and paths down eerie canyons, dizzy high ridge itineraries and a host of walkers' peaks. This guide provides

The Piano Grande below Castelluccio (Walk 19)

a selection of 21 day walks ranging from 1hr 30mins to 6hrs in duration, and covering the unmissable features of this region. In addition, a magnificent 8-day trek circling the Sibillini is given in detail: the GAS – Grande Anello dei Sibillini – is highly recommended and accessible to everyone, as nothing of a mountaineering nature is required. Created by enthusiasts from the Italian Alpine Club in the 1980s, it dips in and out of peaceful out-of-the-way hamlets. The objective was to offer an overall vision of the Sibillini and involve outermost villages, a superb idea. Moreover, it encourages visitors to discover that there is more to the Sibilllini than the hot spots such as Castelluccio and Gole dell'Infern-accio, where visitor numbers are huge at peak times. The GAS lends itself to numerous variations as well as detours to link up with the shorter day walks.

For Italian readers the landmark work is *Monti Sibillini. Parco Nazionale. Le più belle escursioni.* (SER/CAI 2004), by pioneers Alberico Alesi and Maurizio Calibani. This is a comprehensive guide to the park's pathways and environmental concerns, with copious background titbits.

WHEN TO GO

Walkers can count on stepping out on Sibillini pathways from spring well into autumn, the drawn-out season being a great bonus for nature lovers and outdoor enthusiasts. The outermost, lower altitude districts such as those covered by the GAS are often accessible as early as April, though that will depend on how much snow is still lying around from winter as it can obscure important waymarks. The *rifugi* used on that route are owned by the park authority and are theoretically open from mid-April through to mid-October. The late spring months guarantee amazing spreads of wildflowers. On the other hand, to explore the higher ridges and routes in the heart of the Sibillini it's best to wait until June for optimum conditions. Midsummer – August, and weekends in particular – tends to be synonymous with overcrowding at key spots such as Castelluccio and Lago di Pilato. Then too, extreme heat may

RAINFALL AND TEMPERATURE READINGS

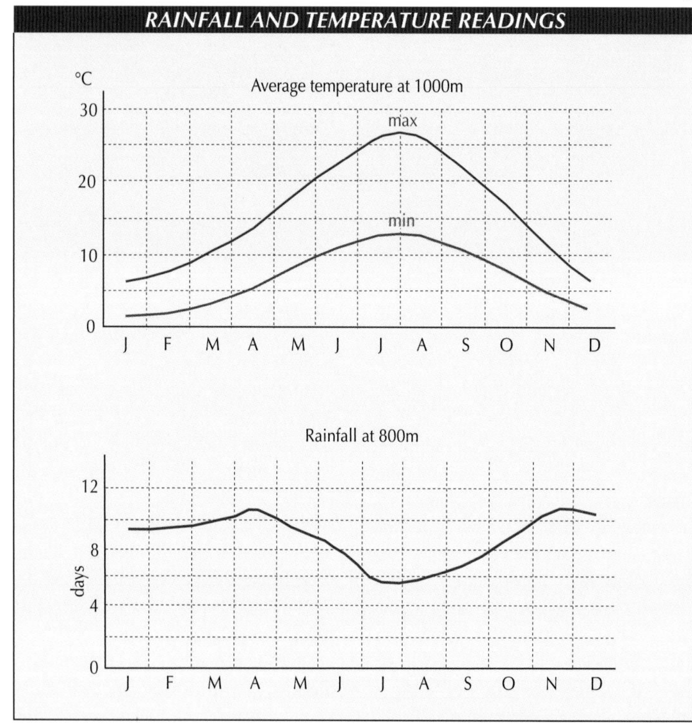

Pian Piccolo and autumn mist (Walk 20)

be followed by thunderstorms. On the other hand, in September–October, clear crisp conditions and stable weather generally prevail, brilliant for walking. Daylight lasts until 6pm even as late as the final weeks of October, after which Italy reverts to normal time after a long summer on daylight saving time. Lastly, wintertime can be magical for exploring these mountains with snowshoes or touring skis, perhaps with a local guide.

WEATHER NOTES

As the 19th-century American poet W.C. Byrant put it so adroitly in his poem *To the Apennines*: 'There the winds no barrier know'. Be prepared for amazingly strong one-way winds that come howling in from the west and the Tyrrhenian coast and batter the Sibillini leaving little upright – walkers included – before heading over to the Adriatic coast. These conditions are prohibitive and to embark on ridge routes on such days is not just inadvisable but downright dangerous. A positive legacy of this nuisance is the stunning visibility and long-distance views left in its aftermath. Another meteorological phenomenon not be under-rated is mist and low cloud. This can transform even the easiest trail into a trying exercise in orienteering. What's more, wet grass can be slippery. The Piano Grande zone is especially prone, though the upside is atmospheric photographs for those who are patient enough.

Handy meteorological websites with forecasts and webcams are www.umbriameteo.com and http://meteo.regione.marche.it/assam.

ACCESS

Air: *(See map on page 7.)* For the Sibillini the most convenient places to fly into are the airports on the Adriatic coast: Ancona and Pescara are served by RyanAir (www.ryanair.com), while Rimini's flights come courtesy of Easyjet (www.easyjet.com). A good distance inland is Perugia, another handy arrival point thanks to recent services by Ryanair. Also fairly convenient are Rome's two airports: Fiumicino (flights by British Airways www.ba.com) and Ciampino, which is served by both the above-mentioned low cost companies. All have bus connections to railway stations.

Trains and Buses: Public transport is a wonderful way to travel anywhere as it gives a privileged insight into a different way of life and facilitates encounters with the locals. While sometimes slower and less flexible than self-driving, it means passengers don't have to worry about missing a turn-off and are free to enjoy the wonderful scenery. Services are reliable and fares reasonable thanks to state subsidies. Last, but definitely not least, it discourages visitors from introducing more polluting vehicles into the wonderful Italian countryside. Don't believe anyone who tells you that public transport is not feasible – this guide was researched using it! While not every corner of the Sibillini can be reached in this way, remember that most villages have someone on hand to act as a taxi driver – ask at the local café or bar. Moreover don't hesitate to request a lift from your hotel or *rifugio*, as most willingly ferry guests to and from bus stops and walk starts.

Generally speaking the Sibillini are pretty well serviced by buses, though sections wholly lacking in links are the central valley between Castelsantangelo and Castelluccio, and the key road pass Forca di Presta above Arquata del Tronto. Connections between the tiny villages on the eastern flanks are not especially straightforward either.

Train is a good way to approach the Sibillini, followed by the inevitable transfer to a bus. The railway can be used in Umbria as far as Terni on the main Rome–Florence artery (then a bus to Visso), or to Spoleto, for a bus to Norcia. In the Marche there's the Civitanova Marche–Fabriano line: get off at Castelraimondo for a bus to Camerino (10km), a key transport hub. Further south, another branch line on the Adriatic coast reaches Ascoli Piceno.

- Italian railways (FS Ferrovie dello Stato) (☎ 892021 or www.trenitalia.com

Beneath Monte Castel Manardo (GAS, Stage 3)

The Monte Vettore ridge (GAS, Stage 6)

- Contram buses (☎ 800 037737 or www.contram.it (click on *orari* for timetables) covers the north-eastern Sibillini with year-round lines branching out from Camerino to Visso, Castelsantangelo sul Nera, Fiastra, Bolognola. Midsummer extensions include Frontignano (from Visso) and direct services to the Adriatic coast and Pesaro. Moreover there's a handy daily run via Visso to Rome.
- Mazzuca ☎ 0736 402267 or www.mazzuca.it covers the Aso valley, Montemonaco and Amandola to Ascoli Piceno.
- SASP ☎ 0733 663137 links Camerino with Sarnano and Amandola.
- Umbria Mobilità ☎ 800 512141 or www.umbriamobilita.it is responsible for connecting Norcia with Rome, Spoleto and Preci as well as the Thursdays-only service to Castelluccio.
- Start ☎ 800 443040 or www.startspa.it links Balzo and the Montegallo district with Ascoli Piceno.

Important note: hardly any buses run on Sundays or public holidays except in midsummer.

These terms may come in handy: *giornaliero* (abbreviated as G) means daily, *scolastico* during school term, *feriale* Mon–Sat, and *festivo* Sunday or public holidays, while *sciopero* is strike.

EXPLORING THE SIBILLINI

The way you travel around the Sibillini will depend on how much time you have and individual preferences for walking. Visitors with no time constraints will enjoy riding the buses and meandering around the park, criss-crossing it with a combination of walking routes and staying at different places. The multi-day GAS trek is easily accessed with public transport. However, those with limited time are best using their own vehicle to cover as much ground as possible. The following notes explain the layout of the Sibillini and the facilities for visitors.

The Sibillini are embraced by an inter-connecting web of narrow valleys settled with small townships and villages. All have accommodation in the shape of welcoming hotels and cosy B&Bs as well as a restaurant or two, and make a good base for forays into the rugged mountainous core.

Beginning in the east, in the rural atmosphere of the Marche region, historic settlements dot the gently rolling slopes that begin at the foot of Monte Vettore and Sibilla and continue all the way to the Adriatic coast. The attractive red-brick town of Amandola, named for an ancient almond tree (*mandorlo*), is a handy gateway to the park from the north-east. It enjoys good transport links and tourist facilities, not to mention excellent mountain views from its belvedere. A short distance inland is Campolungo and Walk 5, while another detour leads to Rubbiano for Walk 9. Not far south is quiet, walled Montemonaco, founded by pioneer Benedictine monks in the very early middle ages. It stands at the foot of Monte Sibilla, at whose *rifugio* Walk 10 begins. The GAS trek passes close by, while a narrow side valley climbs to the mountain hamlet of Foce and Walk 15. The next notable settlement is Montegallo, actually a scatter of villages that go by this collective name. Here, beautifully situated Balzo is low key but well equipped for visitors, and acts as an alternative stopover for the GAS.

Now a winding road climbs south, high above the turrets and colonnades of landmark Arquata del Tronto on the ancient Roman artery, the Via Salaria. Veering west, this strategic road passes Forca di Presta, whose *rifugio* is a transit point for the GAS and start for Walks 17 and 20. A separate branch from Arquata del Tronto leads to Forca Canapine with accommodation and access to both Walk 21 and the GAS. Forking north from here, a minor road traverses the wondrous and unworldly Piano Grande to Castelluccio. This jumble of tumble-down houses occupies a hilltop belvedere that swarms with visitors during the *fiorita* in early June, when the lentil fields explode with wildflowers. Advance booking for accommodation is recommended then. It does have a bus service – on Thursdays – when the gregarious Castelluccio housewives ride down to Norcia for the weekly market.

Preci cascades down a hillside (Walk 13)

Walks 14, 16, 18 and 19 start at Castelluccio.

Norcia is another key gateway to the Sibillini and has fine tourist facilities and good bus links. Sometimes called Nursia in English, the town's name comes from Northia, Goddess of Fortune, venerated by the Etruscans. This relaxed, charming town is set amidst vast farming plains on the easternmost edge of Umbria. Best known as the birthplace of high profile St Benedict, founder of the Benedictine monastic movement, for Italians it is also famous for *norcineria* or the noble art of sausage and salami making. Shop fronts are draped with strings of tasty specimens and even family names reflect the ancient trade (such as Ansuini, from 'swine'). Though a little out of the way for the bulk of the walks, Norcia is handy for Walk 14.

A minor road via Forca d'Ancarano goes to peaceful Preci, on the park's western edge, where lovely old houses cascade down a steep hillside. With good accommodation and bus links, it is the base for Walk 13. From Preci drivers can loop via canyon-like Nera valley to Visso (see below).

From Castelluccio a road continues northwest to the pass Forca di Gualdo, aka Madonna della Cona, where a detour east terminates at Monte Prata and its hotel, the start of Walk 11. The pass marks an entrance into the inner heart of the Sibillini, a dramatically contrasting world of dense woods of beech, oak and chestnut which provide cover for many animals. Here, deep, plunging valleys are surrounded by bare-topped mountains. The road drops in tight zigzags to the valley floor and Castelsantangelo sul Nera. Quite central to the park area, this charming place has a heritage of monasteries and castles whose fortifications straggle up the mountainside forming an inverted 'V'. Nera may derive from *narici* or nostrils, a reference to the two holes in the rock at the base of the spring where the eponymous river rises. Adjacent Valle Infante is fast becoming a favourite haunt for both deer and elusive wolves. Nearby Nocelleto and its guesthouse is the start of Walk 12. A minor road climbs to the modest ski resort of Frontignano. Dominated by Monte Bove it has hotels and Walk 8. The road then descends to Ussita.

From Castelsantangelo, the steep-sided, poplar-lined Valnerina proceeds northwest, alongside the river which feeds a mineral water bottling plant and trout farm. The next landmark is attractive Visso, which has a well-preserved historic centre and is the HQ of the Sibillini National Park. Old castles stand out on the surrounding mountainsides while stern, carved stone gateways open onto the town's late medieval heart with its lovely Romanesque churches and paved alleys. Set at the confluence of three valleys and consequently three gushing rivers, Visso was repeatedly flooded and in the mid-1800s an expert engineer had to be called in – from Venice, no less. Torrente Ussita, the offending watercourse, now flows obediently through an artificial channel, which makes for a curious sight. Visso is the official start of the GAS trek, and has decent bus services, shops and tourist facilities.

Off to the east in a river valley with dizzy cliffsides stands Ussita, reachable by bus. The road continues up the valley to Casali, a pretty hamlet with accommodation, at the base of Monte Bove Nord and a convenient base for Walk 6. A motorable lane climbs to Forcella del Fargno and Walk 7.

From Visso a busy road climbs north towards Camerino, with branches soon turning off for Fiastra and its lake. This scatter of hamlets, including low-key lakeside tourist facilities, serves as a stopover on the GAS, as well as the start of Walk 2. Walk 1 can be accessed from Monastero, a short drive northeast.

Penetrating the inner Sibillini, a winding road leads southeast to Bolognola with its decent tourist amenities. Its name is believed to derive from Bologna, as it was founded by three exiled families from the north. Another theory claims links with Bona, worshipped by the ancient Sabini people as protector of fertility for land and women alike. Now a small, sleepy settlement, it was once immensely important for the wool trade. Walks 3 and 4 begin in the village itself, while up a dirt road climbing south, at Forcella del Fargno, is the start of Walk 7.

From M Vettore to Pizzo del Diavolo and Lago di Pilato (Walk 17)

INFORMATION

In addition to the website for the Parco Nazionale dei Monti Sibillini (www.sibillini.net), Visitors' Centres (referred to as *Case del Parco*) operate through the summer months. Information is on offer at park headquarters at Visso (☎ 0737 95219), as well as Amandola (☎ 0736 848598), Castelsantangelo sul Nera (☎ 073798152), Fiastra (☎ 0737 52185), Montemonaco (☎ 0736 856462), Norcia (☎ 0743 817090), Preci (☎ 0743 937000) and Ussita (☎ 0737 99190) among others.

Norcia also has a general tourist office (☎ 0743 828173, www.norcia.net). An excellent resource for the Marche region is English-language website www.le-marche.com, free-phone (from Italy) ☎ 800 222111. For Umbria visit www.english.umbria2000.it.

HOW TO USE THIS GUIDE

The headings for each walk give:

Walking Time: this does not include pauses for picnics, admiring views, photos and nature stops, so always add on a couple of hours to be realistic.

Difficulty: Grade 1 means a straightforward route on mostly level ground, with no difficulty. Grade 2 is suitable

Above Fonte delle Cacere (GAS, Stage 6)

for reasonably fit walkers with minimum mountain experience. (The long-distance GAS is rated Grade 2.) Tackling a Grade 3 route is inadvisable for beginners as it may entail exposed passages and/or orientation problems. That said, everyone should bear in mind that adverse weather such as mist and low visibility, strong wind or rain, can increase difficulty making even a Grade 1 path downright dangerous. Common sense is the best rule.

Ascent/Descent: those accustomed to alpine terrain will appreciate the importance of this figure, especially when it is taken into consideration alongside timing and distance. For instance an ascent of 300m in 1hr is fairly leisurely, whereas 600m in the same time means you can expect to be puffing hard up a pretty steep slope.

Distance: an approximate measure of the walk length.

In the walk descriptions 'road' means the way is surfaced and used by cars, while 'track' and 'lane' are unsurfaced and traffic is limited to farm or forestry vehicles. 'Path' always refers to a pedestrians-only route.

Compass bearings are given (N, SW, NNW and so forth), as is right (R) and left (L). Useful landmarks appear in **bold** type and these are shown on the sketch maps. Their altitude is given in metres (100m=328ft) abbreviated as 'm', not to be confused with minutes (min).

EMERGENCIES

If an accident happens or an emergency arises, if possible phone *soccorso alpino* (mountain rescue) on ☎ 118, supplying them with details of your whereabouts and the nature of the problem. Otherwise summon assistance using the internationally recognised signals: the call for help is SIX signals per minute. These can be visual (such as waving a handkerchief or flashing a torch) or audible (whistling or shouting). They are to be repeated after a one-minute pause. The answer is THREE visual or audible signals per minute, to be repeated after a one-minute pause. Anyone who sees or hears such a call for help must contact the nearest *rifugio*, police station or the like as fast as possible as it may save someone's life.

'Help' is *aiuto* in Italian (pronounced *eye-yoo-toh*) and 'I need help' is *Ho bisogno di aiuto*. The general emergency telephone number in Italy is ☎ 113, but calls for *soccorso alpino* (mountain rescue) are best made to ☎ 118.

The following arm signals could be useful for communicating with a helicopter:

Both arms raised

- Help needed
- Land here
- YES (to pilot's questions)

One arm raised diagonally, one arm down diagonally

- Help not needed
- Do not land here
- NO (to pilot's questions)

If you need non-urgent medical assistance ask at your hotel for the *guardia medica* (24-hour doctor), or go to *pronto soccorso* (emergency) at the nearest *ospedale* (hospital).

Insurance is strongly recommended. Those from the EU need a European Health Insurance Card (EHIC), which has replaced the old E111. Holders are entitled to free or subsidised emergency health treatment in Italy. UK residents can apply online at www.dh.gov.uk ('EHIC and health advice for travellers' section). Travel insurance to cover a walking holiday

Passo Sasso Borghese, Redentore and Vettore peaks from Monte Porche (Walk 11)

is also a good idea as rescue operations incur hefty charges. Members of alpine clubs are usually covered by insurance through their club. British residents can join the UK branch of the Austrian Alpine Club (www.aacuk.org.uk or ☎ 01707 386740) or the British Mountaineering Council (www.the-bmc.co.uk or ☎ 0870 0104878).

MAPS

In combination with a compass, a detailed topographical map showing natural features is essential for exploring the Sibillini on foot. The sketch maps in this guide are only intended as a rough guide and are limited by space restrictions. Hopefully all walks will go well, however in adverse weather conditions such as low cloud with limited visibility, orientation can become a real problem as landmarks are few and far between and a clear map comes into its own.

The best walking map by far is the new 2013 edition of the 'Parco Nazionale dei Monti Sibillini' scale 1:25,000, published by SER (Società Editrice Ricerche). It is on sale throughout the park and neighbouring towns, and can also be ordered from www.edizioniser.com. Kompass also do a decent 1:50,000 walking map – map 666 *Monti Sibillini* – which is available in many overseas outlets. It obviously has less detail, but the smaller size makes it handier to use. Be warned however that Walks 1 and 2 are missing from it, as is a chunk of the GAS Stage 3. The park authorities have also published a new 1:40,000 map (2012), which shows the park routes marked in red and other CAI paths in blue. It is on sale locally but can be downloaded free from the Sibillini Park website at www.sibillini.net.

Users of GPS will be pleased to know that the waypoints relevant to the long-distance trek GAS described in this guide can also be downloaded from www.sibillini.net.

WAYMARKING

The long-distance Grande Anello dei Sibillini (GAS) is well marked throughout with red/white paint stripes on prominent rocks and trees, in addition to low wooden poles and clear signposts at most junctions. A 'G' is usually included. Recently local authorities and the park have been waymarking routes with red/white paint and placing new signposts at landmark junctions. Note: the park has seen fit to mark its own routes with a red 'E' (for 'escursionismo', walking) and short identifying number. Several of these routes coincide with the walks described here so extra signs can be expected. There are also short nature trails (N) and MTB (B) routes. Paths in Umbria were recently renumbered – the initial '1' changed to '5'.

A warning: don't be misled by the optimism of the commercial maps which show an extensive network of lovely routes in red flagged with identifying numbers. On the ground very few are so clearly marked and whether or not an actual path exists is another story. Moreover, in the high areas of the Sibillini above the tree line, with no landmarks, this task is more difficult. In any case, where a clear path exists, it's good practice to follow it and help establish the trail, rather than wandering willy-nilly over grassy slopes and encouraging erosion. Some main routes have red/white identifying marks in accordance with the Italian system of paths of CAI. On the other hand where numbering and markings do exist, this is always explained in the walk description.

Waymarking for GAS trek (below) and Sibillini National Park signposts (right)

WHAT TO TAKE

How do you find that perfect balance between what's essential, and potentially life-saving, and what only adds unnecessary weight to your rucksack and detracts from enjoyment of your holiday? This is an especially important issue for walkers on the GAS trek. Day walkers have it easier, but should still pack for a range of conditions.

A suggested check list for walking the GAS:

- Comfortable rucksack: when packed pop it on the bathroom scales – 8–10kg is a reasonable cut-off point. Plastic bags come in handy for organising the contents.
- Sturdy walking boots, preferably not brand new and with a good gripping sole and ankle support. Sandals or lightweight footwear for the evening.
- Rain-proof gear, either a full poncho or jacket, over-trousers and rucksack cover. A lightweight folding umbrella is a godsend for walkers who wear glasses on the trail.
- Layers of clothing to cope with conditions ranging from biting cold winds through to scorching sun, so T-shirts, short and long trousers, warm fleece and a windproof jacket, as well as a woolly hat and gloves.
- Sun hat, sunglasses, chapstick and high-factor sunblock (remember that the sun's rays become stronger by 10% for every 1000m in ascent). Shade is a rare commodity above the 1500m mark so go prepared.
- Personal toiletries.
- Emergency food such as muesli bars, biscuits and chocolate.
- Walking maps and compass.
- Whistle for calling for help.
- Torch or headlamp and spare batteries.
- An altimeter, handy for understanding weather trends: if the reading at a known altitude (such as a building) begins to rise, a low pressure trough may be approaching, a warning to walkers.
- Trekking poles to ease rucksack weight, aid wonky knees and keep sheep dogs at a safe distance.
- Sleeping sheet (bag liner) and small towel for stays in *rifugi*.
- First-aid kit.
- Lightweight binoculars and camera.
- Supply of euros in cash and credit card.
- Mobile phone, adaptor and recharger. Don't let a mobile lull you into a false sense of security in the mountains. Never expect total signal cover; you won't get it. Don't take risks thinking that if worst comes to the worst you can call for assistance.
- Water bottle – the plastic mineral water containers widely available in Italy are perfect.

Fresh spring water, a boon for thirsty walkers

Note: despite the widespread limestone rock base in the Sibillini, a remarkable number of life-giving springs can be found. Essential to generations of herders for watering their flocks at remote pastures, for walkers the *fonti* (springs) offer delicious cool refreshment during a hot summer. Springs are marked on maps with a blue water droplet.

However, they can not always be relied upon as prolonged dry weather and channelling for local water supplies have diminished flows. Moral: always carry an abundant supply of drinking water.

ACCOMMODATION

There's a good scattering of reasonably priced family-run hotels, cosy guesthouses and a couple of *rifugi* walkers' huts across the Sibillini. In this guide each walk comes complete with contact details of handy places to stay.

The long-distance GAS trek uses mostly *rifugi* – hostels set in quiet hamlets. Without exception these are excellent structures owned by the park authority – mostly modernised, converted farm buildings which operate by contract from approximately mid-April through to mid-October. They have nice dormitories, hot showers and provide all meals, including packed lunches on request. Bed linen and towels are available for a few extra euros for those who prefer to carry a little less weight. Always phone ahead to reserve your bed, especially early and late in the season as some shut up ahead of schedule. Moreover, at quiet times the kitchen may close for a rest day, though staff will redirect guests to a neighbourhood restaurant.

Other privately-operated *rifugi* come in handy in the Sibillini – examples are tiny Rifugio Città di Amandola on the eastern slopes, convivial Rifugio degli Alpini at the Forca di Presta road pass, and helpful Rifugio Casali at the base of Monte Bove Nord, without forgetting spartan but strategically located Rifugio Fargno. These too have dorm accommodation, hot showers and meals, unless specified otherwise. Be aware that maps show other huts with the *rifugio* denomination – such as Rifugio Zilioli on Monte Vettore and Capanna Ghezzi out of Castelluccio. Old herders' huts, basic and unmanned, they belong to CAI for its members – see Walks 16 and 17 for contact info.

Additionally a number of hotels of varying categories are listed. Many offer a half-board (*mezza pensione*) option which covers your overnight stay plus a three-course dinner (drinks may not be included) and continental breakfast. Off season it's worth enquiring about special offers or lower rates, as occupancy out of the July–August period is not exactly sky high.

If your Italian isn't up to phone calls, once in the Sibillini it's a good idea to get *rifugio* or hotel staff to phone to book your accommodation for the days ahead. But do remember to cancel bookings if your plans change! Should the need arise, don't hesitate to ask to be picked up from – or dropped off at – the nearest town or bus stop. Some establishments will do it as a favour to guests but assume it's a taxi service and offer payment.

Accommodation on offer

Hotel Felycita at Frontignano (Walk 8)

If you wish to set off early in the morning – usually a good idea in hot weather – settle your bill in the evening, and see if the staff where you are staying are prepared to leave a breakfast tray and thermos out for you.

In general do not assume anyone accepts credit cards and have a supply of euro cash on hand. Main towns including Balzo di Montegallo, Fiastra, Norcia, Visso and Castelsantangelo have ATMs.

If you don't mind carrying the extra weight, camping out is a wonderful way to explore the Sibillini and gives you the chance to spend more time in the high places. While it is officially forbidden in the realms of the park, it is tolerated for discrete single overnight stays from dusk to dawn. Otherwise base yourself at one of the camping grounds listed here:

- Balzo di Montegallo: Camping Vettore, Strada San Nicola 15 ☎ 0736 807007 open Easter to early Jan www.campingvettore.it
- Calcara near Ussita: TGS Amici Colorito ☎ 0737 99443, and Estate Inverno ☎ 0737 99448.
- Castelvecchio near Preci: Campeggio Il Collaccio ☎ 0743 939005, open April–Sept www.ilcollaccio.com
- Fiastra: Campeggio al Lago ☎ 0737 52295
- Schianceto above Castelsantangelo sul Nera: Camping Monte Prata ☎ 0737 970062, open 15/6–15/9, www.campingmonteprata.it

Shopping for lunch at Visso market

FOOD AND DRINK

Pasta is the natural starting point for this important section. Proudly home-made fresh ribbons or luscious thin strips feature high on menus as *tagliatelle* or *tagliolini*. Smothering sauces include *funghi* (local wild mushrooms, unfailingly delicious), *ragù*, hearty meat sauce, and *amatriciana*, a spicy stew of *pancetta* (bacon), tomatoes and onions. Meat is naturally high-profile food in these mountainous areas, notably as a *secondo* course. Wild boar (*cinghiale*) may be offered *in umido* (stewed). Don't be put off by the offer of *castrato* which means a type of tender lamb. Delicious when barbecued and sprinkled with herbs and olive oil, it is eaten with the hands. *Grigliata mista* is mixed grilled meat, generally *pollo* (chicken), *manzo* (beef), *agnello* (lamb) or older *pecora* (mutton), while *rosticini* are barbecued skewers of whatever meat is going. *Olive ascolane* from the Ascoli Piceno district are fat green olives stuffed with sausage meat, crumbed, fried and devoured finger-burning hot!

The Piano Grande di Castelluccio is famous all over Italy for its tiny flavoursome lentils, *lenticchie* (yes, Italians do get excited about such little things if it's related to eating). They may be served in a savoury runny soup consumed with toasted unsalted bread or accompanied by spicy sausages. On the vegetable front (*contorno*, side dish) there is bitter *cicoria*, wild greens that are boiled lightly then tossed in garlic, chilli and oil. Autumn walkers have a good chance of being fed hot roast or boiled *castagne* (chestnuts).

Cheese (*formaggio*) tends to be dominated by *pecorino* (sheep's milk cheese) though blends using cow's milk (*latte di mucca*) are common. A variant on the delicious soft Italian *ricotta* cheese is creamy *raviggiolo*, consumed fresh or used in pasta stuffing as well as desserts. Evidently records survive from the 1500s when it was presented as a prized gift to the Pope.

In the Marche region aniseed (*anice*) is a common ingredient, and is used effectively with red wine in fragrant, baked *biscotti*. It is also the main ingredient of Varnelli, a very popular clear spirit, a bit like Pastis. A delicious dessert wine that is home-made and can be exceedingly sweet is *vino cotto*, with shades of Marsala. Wines vary tremendously though reds tend to dominate. If you're after booze from the surrounding territory, the Marche has a couple of DOC raters (*Dominazione di Origine controllata*, an essential guarantee): Rosso Piceno is a very decent table quality, best drunk young, and a white equivalent is Falerio dei Colli Ascolani. Umbrian wines from the vicinity include Colli Martani and Colli Amerini varieties. Naturally, serious wine lists also feature vintages from leading Italian regions such as Tuscany and Piemonte.

Breakfast (*prima colazione*) is a choice of *té* (tea), *caffé* served with *latte* (milk) or frothed up as a *cappuccino*, or just short, strong and black (*nero*) in *espresso* form. Children can often request *cioccolata calda* (hot chocolate), but parents should be aware that this rich dense luscious Italian version is highly addictive! Bread, butter and jam (*pane, burro, marmellata*) complete the picture, maybe a pastry if you're lucky.

PLANT LIFE

As is immediately obvious, the tree line in the Sibillini is virtually at a clear cut 1500m above sea level. The entire range was once thickly forested with beech and fir, but demands of livestock rearing and nomadic grazers, along with charcoal burners, progressively led to widespread deforestation, resulting in vast expanses of grassland on upper slopes. However, swathes of thick woodland persist at medium altitudes, a stunning spectacle in autumn with infinite shades of red and orange.

The flower arena is vast and extremely exciting for enthusiasts, as a remarkably broad array of blooms flourish thanks to the marvellous diversity of habitats. These embrace a range from low-altitude dry and typically Mediterranean terrains, woodland, pasture slopes, all the way up to alpine-like altitudes well over 2000m. There's also a decent batch of 'endemics' – plants found in a limited geographical area. Most notably, the elevated central ridges of the Sibillini are the perfect haunt for the rare Apennine edelweiss. Like its

Wild peonies

Trumpet gentians on high slopes

The curious Eryngo bloom

Orange lily

Type of alpine cabbage on scree

The divine bee orchid

iconic alpine relative it has creamy-coloured thick velvet petals and pale green leaves. However, this plant grows closer to the ground, presumably to protect itself from the strong winds prevalent here. It begins flowering in late June and is a protected species! Brilliant blue gentians share its habitat along with delicate pink rock jasmine and lilac alpine asters. Not far away on limestone scree are golden poppies and clumps of fleshy-leafed alpine cabbage, yellow and attractive despite the name. A little further down at meadow altitude flourish a wealth of divine orchids, including the exquisite insect types known as *Ophrys*. Elegant orange lilies and the wine-red martagon variety are never far away. Shady woods on the other hand are the perfect place for batches of deep crimson peonies.

Colouring bare fields with pretty splashes of violet-blue along its stem and prickly flower heads, a variety of *Eryngo*, a curious slender thistle is commonly seen all the way through to the autumn months. It is known romantically in Italian as *Cardo di Venere*, 'Venus thistle'. Sun-beaten hillsides at lower altitudes are often colonised by typical Mediterranean vegetation comprising light woods with holm oak and bushes of sweet broom. Masses of aromatic herbs line pathways, their distinctive scent wafting through the air. Mint, oregano and smell-alikes thyme and piquant savory are the most common, along with the distinctive curry plant *Helichrysum* with woolly yellow blooms.

However in terms of flowers, the most famous spot in the Sibillini and indeed in the whole of Italy, is the Piano Grande di Castelluccio. This huge unique upland basin is an explosion of colour in late spring. Fields where lentil crops have been planted are painted with immense watercolour strokes as wildflowers such as poppies, cornflowers, vetch, mustard and myriad others come out. It is celebrated as the *Fiorita* and usually happens in early June. (See also Walk 19.)

The interesting Giardino Botanico Appeninico is only a short stroll above Visso (on the GAS trail). Helpful handbooks are Christopher Grey-Wilson and Marjorie Blamey's *Alpine Flowers of Britain and Europe* (HarperCollins, 1995) as well as Thomas Schauer and Claus Caspari's *A Field Guide to the Wild Flowers of Britain and Europe* (Collins, 1982).

WILDLIFE

A remarkable variety of wild animals call the Monti Sibillini their home, though most remain elusive to the casual visitor. At best, walkers can expect an interesting range of birds.

The vast expanses of hillsides covered with low grass are the perfect habitat for ground-nesting rock partridge, which take off in small flocks with a cluttering of wings and heart-stopping guttural clucks if surprised.

Apennine chamois with its distinctive long horns

They fly somewhat clumsily for short distances, keeping quite close to the ground. Far above, kestrel and buzzards circle, and four pairs of nesting eagles have been reported. The Piano Grande is excellent for birdwatching.

The Apennine chamois (*Rupicapra pyrenaica ornata*), a fleet-footed, nimble mountain goat, is being reintroduced in stages to the Monti Sibillini. A small group inhabits a special enclosure at Bolognola, in semi-captivity but slated for release, while successful re-introductions have been made on Monte Bove. The total population in the Italian Apennines is at 800, so this initiative is being carefully – and optimistically – monitored. They differ from their northern alpine cousin in having much longer horns, but with the same crochet hook. See Walk 4 for details.

Marsican bears, smaller than grizzlies and native to the central Apennines, have been making forays from neighbouring Abruzzo into the heart of the Monti Sibillini of late. The local population of *Ursus arctos marsicanus* became extinct in the 1800s, but monitoring for droppings and pawprints begun in 2006 has confirmed a fleeting presence. Camera traps are also used, with encouraging results. There is evidence of at least one bear hibernating here. In all, a mere 40 bears survive in Italy's Apennine parks, under serious threat from man – poison bait is not unknown.

There is also exciting news about wolves in the area. Censuses carried out using the technique of wolf-howling confirm that 20 wolves currently

Orsini's viper, a rare sighting

roam the park. Similar to a German shepherd dog, with a reddish-brown coat and grey overtones, *Canis lupus talicus* is a tad smaller than his North American counterpart; a full-grown male can weigh up to 35kg and a female 25kg. The wolves' favourite prey are deer, though they do not disdain hares, birds and rodents.

Roe deer are fairly common in the woods, and a recent project saw the re-introduction of 49 magnificent red deer from Tarvisio in the northern Italian Alps. Concentrated in the thickly forested central valleys of the park near Castelsantangelo sul Nera, several of them wear radio collars to enable zoologists to track them. The Park Visitor Centre there also manages an enclosure for animals in need of temporary assistance.

Shy wild boars feast on nuts and fruit in the beech woods, which also provide good cover. Evidence of their presence comes in the form of excrements, hoofprints and mud baths. Prolific breeders, they have been introduced all the way down the Italian peninsula by hunting enthusiasts though they are protected within the park confines. The newcomers have replaced the native type, smaller in size and less fertile.

A couple of snakes live in the Sibillini, the common viper or adder being the only potentially dangerous one. Light brown-grey with broad stripes or a zigzag pattern on its body, they sometimes hang around abandoned buildings in the hope of rodents for dinner. Sluggish in the morning until solar recharging takes effect (they often sunbathe on paths), they need time to slither away and only attack walkers when they feel threatened. Though painful, their bite is rarely fatal. However it should not be under-rated; speedy medical assistance is imperative. While awaiting help, the victim should be kept calm and still, and the affected limb bandaged to restrict circulation.

On the other hand a rare treat is Orsini's viper, found solely in the central Apennines. Smaller, with attractive diamond markings, this harmless snake feeds on grasshoppers.

Two tiny crustaceans breed in the rare Sibillini lakes – and nowhere else in the world. The most famous is *Chirocephalus marchesonii*, a unique freshwater fairy shrimp discovered in 1954 and probably destined to disappear along with its home, Lago di Pilato which is rapidly shrinking (it once dried up completely, in 1990). The creature's eggs are laid on the water's edge and can evidently survive a year at a time while the shrimp itself needs to be immersed in water – see Walk 15 for more.

Lastly, be warned that sheep dogs occasionally pose problems. Do remember that they're just doing their job and see walkers as intruders in their territory. Keep your distance as they have been known to attack outsiders. Under *no* circumstances bring a dog of your own – even on a leash – as they can disturb the wild animals that rely on these mountains for their home and survival.

Raised river at Visso (GAS, Stage 1)

THE GAS: GRANDE ANELLO DEI SIBILLINI

This rewarding 8-day trek, designed as a 120km ring route around the perimeter of the marvellous Sibillini park, gives an excellent idea of the dramatic mountain range. Long days are spent on wild hillsides overlooking vast plains and thickly forested valleys, the stages differing excitingly one from another. The Grande Anello, the 'great ring', referred to in Italian as l'Anello, can be interrupted virtually on a daily basis so that walkers can embark on variants to places of great interest in the innermost heart of the Sibillini. For instance the Gole dell'Infernaccio is visitable from Rubbiano (Stage 4), and the range's highest peak, Monte Vettore, can be climbed from Forca di Presta (Stage 6). One warmly recommended alternative veers off the official route at Forca di Presta to cross the Piano Grande to the iconic hillside village of Castelluccio, a must-see. From there a short leg returns to the GAS.

The walking is straightforward and suitable for everyone, a perfect first experience without the long steep climbs and knee-destroying descents of some of the

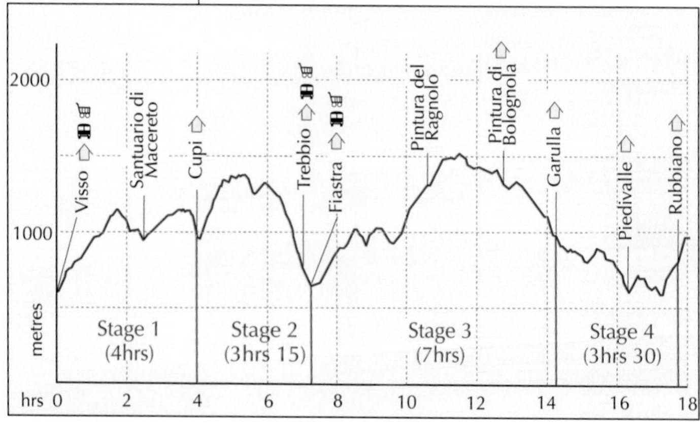

more arduous itineraries in the day walk section of this guide. In terms of grading it rates easy to average with no technical difficulties at all, so an overall Grade 2 applies. Each day concludes satisfactorily at a cosy *rifugio* (walkers' hostel) where guests are well looked after and catered for, and there are a couple of intermediate guesthouses as well if needed. The original plan entailed renovating old village buildings at strategic points en route, and at the time of writing all but one of these excellent park-owned structures – Rubbiano – were operational. The latest information on accommodation can be found on the park website www.sibillini.net.

The route is pretty well marked on the ground with red/white paint stripes and 'G' in green, and there are signposts at most junctions. ▶ Naturally, cows do occasionally knock over signposts, and vegetation can hide marks on rocks so be flexible too.

As a general rule don't proceed for more than 20 minutes without seeing markings.

It is by no means compulsory to begin the trek at Visso: Fiastra in Stage 2 has buses from Camerino, as does Bolognola (below Pintura) in Stage 3. Colle di Montegallo in Stage 5 is a short walk from Balzo, served by bus from Ascoli Piceno, similarly Montemonaco, handy for Isola San Biagio in Stage 5. In the southwestern part Rifugio Perugia in Stage 7 and the Castelluccio

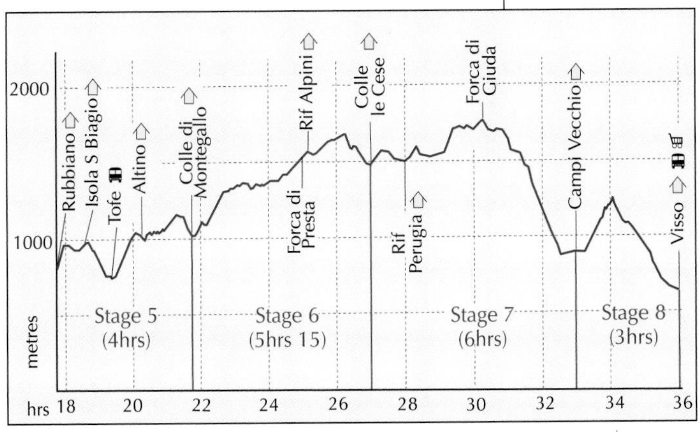

View of Castelluccio

variant can be accessed thanks to the Thursday bus from Norcia. Then Campi Vecchio, also in Stage 7, is close to the Norcia–Preci line. Lastly, don't hesitate to ask for a lift as most *rifugi* and hotels will happily taxi guests to and from nearby towns.

On the way around the GAS get the *rifugi* to stamp (*timbrare*) your notebook or the end pages of this guide. Present these at the park offices and you will be rewarded with a certificate *(attestato)*.

A final note: midsummer walkers are advised to avoid the central hours of the day especially on the eastern section with its low altitudes where it can get pretty hot.

Access to start point: The official start of the GAS is at Visso, served by coach from Camerino, or Rome via Terni.

Visso itself is an attractive historic town that hosts the headquarters of the Sibillini Park, its only downside is the absence of budget accommodation. (See the Introduction for more about Visso.)

Where to stay: In Piazza Capuzzi, friendly B&B Due Torri ☎ 0737 95403 or mobile 338 4226790, or B&B Casa dell'Artista ☎ 0737 9364. Otherwise Hotel Elena ☎ 0737 9277 www.hotelristorantelena.com.

STAGE 1

Visso to Cupi

Time	4hrs
Distance	13km/8.1 miles
Ascent/descent	800m/430m

An enthusiastic start to this wonderful trek, Stage 1 leaves the pretty township of Visso to climb through woods and pastureland towards memorable views of the northernmost Sibillini mountains. A photogenic medieval sanctuary in the middle of nowhere is the star of the stage, which later concludes at a cosy *rifugio* in a tiny farming hamlet.

Note: though it is a pity to miss Cupi, fit walkers will find it feasible to combine Stages 1 and 2 and continue on to Fiastra – only an additional 2hrs 15mins. A marked fork prior to the final descent to Cupi, shows the way.

Starting out from the 'Casa del Parco' Sibillini Visitor Centre at **Visso** (685m), go upstream along the retaining wall of Torrente Ussita then L across the bridge. Follow narrow alleys R then L past the Pettacci delicatessen (and its mouth-watering display of picnic supplies) in Via XXIV Maggio. This leads through to Piazza Capuzzi and the elegant 12th-century Palazzo dei Priori, home to the town council, its facade adorned with enigmatic twin clocks. Turn R along Via Galliano to the northeastern edge of town and the market place. In the L corner 'G' waymarks beneath the arches of an old convent building point up the stepped way Salita Boncompagni, quickly leaving the town precinct. You pass below the 12th-century Rocca, an essential refuge for the town's inhabitants when enemies threatened, and past the Giardino Botanico Appeninico. The path leads NNE high above Torrente Ussita, a constant but never difficult climb in a mixed woodland of deciduous and coniferous trees,

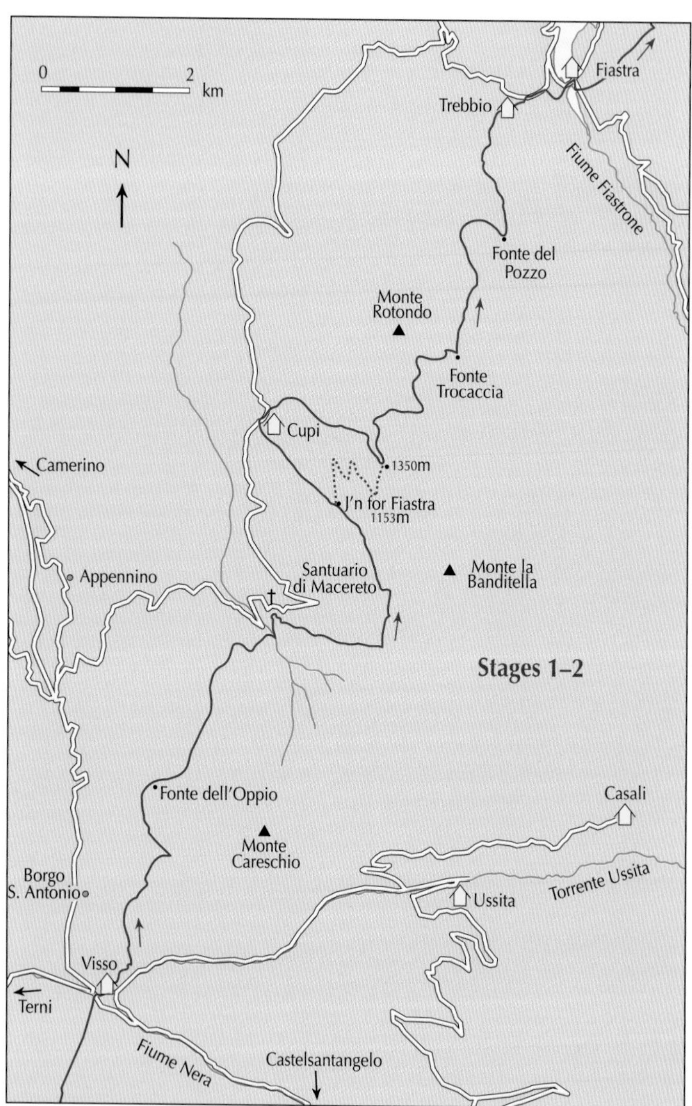
0
2
km
N
Fiastra
Trebbio
Fiume Fiastrone
Fonte del Pozzo
Monte Rotondo
Fonte Trocaccia
Cupi
Camerino
1350m
J'n for Fiastra
1153m
Appennino
Santuario di Macereto
Monte la Banditella
Stages 1–2
Fonte dell'Oppio
Casali
Monte Careschio
Borgo S. Antonio
Ussita
Torrente Ussita
Visso
Terni
Fiume Nera
Castelsantangelo

lovely and peaceful. Through the foliage E is a fleeting glimpse of Monte Bove Nord, the first of the Sibillini peaks to be sighted so far.

The way bears N across Colle della Torre keeping high up in dry Mediterranean holm-oak woodland, thick with dog roses. You cut the western flanks of Monte Careschio and join a wider track on the edge of the park. After **Fonte dell'Oppio** (1017m) a final climb emerges on an exceptionally scenic saddle (1160m) where horses graze amidst juniper bushes. Stark Monte Bove Nord and Monte Priora soar into sight ESE, and downhill you see the sanctuary set on a plain. An easy descent along a lane dips through a minor valley before emerging at photogenic

2hrs 30mins – Santuario di Macereto (1000m). Ensconced in a pine grove miles away from the city of Macereto from which it took its name, the striking octagonal church and surrounding porticoes date back to the mid-1500s. There is nothing else for miles around on this plain. Its presence can be explained by the fact that a busy pilgrim route once came through this way, destination Loreto, the immense sanctuary on the Adriatic coast constructed around the original house of the Virgin Mary (miraculously flown in one night from the Holy Land by angels). The sanctuary marks the spot of a curious incident: a mule carrying a wooden statue of the Holy Mother fell to its knees and would go no further. A deliciously cool spring slakes the thirst of pilgrims and walkers alike.

Turn R up the surfaced road a short distance to where a marked path breaks off L (E) diagonally uphill. It leads across open hillsides dotted with juniper which barely conceal ground-nesting rock partridges and there are more enticing views to the outcrops E. After a drinking trough at 1156m, the route veers N for a long, level traverse beneath modest Monte la Banditella. Several more springs are passed, essential for the livestock encountered on these grassy hillsides. The next useful landmark is

Santuario di Macereto

1hrs 10mins – junction for Fiastra (1153m). This marked fork R (N) is handy if you decide to press on for Fiastra. The lane climbs in wide curves in 20mins to the 1350m mark and the link with the route from Cupi, cutting 1hr off walking time.

Heading NW now, the track descends gradually at first, finally dropping more steeply through light woodland past a water trough to

20mins – Cupi (986m). Nowadays a sleepy rural settlement, it was once the site of a pagan sanctuary for the goddess Cupra. On the corner of the road stands the comfortable *rifugio*. Under young management it earns top marks for its welcoming open fire and fantastic catering. ☎ 0737 971041, sleeps 50, open spring–early Nov, info@asgaia.it. The hamlet itself has a total of 14 permanent inhabitants, shepherds for the most part, and high-level cheese-making goes on. The tiny church dates back to the 12th century.

Cupi

STAGE 2

Cupi to Fiastra

Time	3hrs 15mins
Distance	11.1km/6.9 miles
Ascent/descent	600m/700m

Far from the central peaks, this loop of the GAS leads around the northernmost reaches of the Sibillini and the park. While not exceptionally exciting, it is certainly pleasant and offers a vision of this outlying district. Herding – horses, cows and sheep – is very much in evidence, aided by the copious springs and drinking troughs. The day concludes at the conglomeration of villages that goes under the confusing name of Fiastra. In fact the *rifugio* for this stage is located at the first village encountered en route, Trebbio. Lower down, the lakeside area with visitor facilities is referred to variously as San Lorenzo or simply Fiastra. In any case it is one of the few places on the GAS route that boasts groceries and an ATM. In addition to a wander around the ancient castle ruins at Trebbio, several day walks can be picked up.

Leave **Cupi** (986m) past the church and along the road NE. After a matter of minutes, turn R up a rough lane (signpost L side of road). This soon becomes a faint path with rare waymarks, climbing steadily up the flanks of Costa Tranquilla. At **1350m** you veer abruptly L (N), joined by the direct variant from Stage 1. Initially a wide track then a clear path, it traverses grassy terrain thick with thistles and looks out over undulating grazing hills and rare settlements. Mostly level, with the exception of a minor ridge crossed on Monte Rotondo, the GAS cuts down E to a makeshift farm and **Fonte Troccaccia** (1285m) at the head of Valle di Campobonomo. Here keep your eyes peeled for the faint path cutting NNE through a conifer plantation to a dirt road. This is followed N for the most part across Monte Coglia

Climbing high above Cupi

to antennas and the first inspiring view of Lago di Fiastrone. At **Fonte del Pozzo** (1237m) the GAS leaves the track to cut N down scrubby hillsides thick with wild rose bushes. It descends easily and enters oak and beech woods where pheasants may be spotted. A lane is intersected a couple of times. Soon after signs announcing 'Riserva Tartufi Riservata' (truffle reserve!) is

3hrs – Trebbio (756m) and the *rifugio*, a beautifully restored local building converted into a hostel for walkers and a restaurant (☎ 0737 527027 or mob 333 6733300, www.rifugioditribbio.com, sleeps 18, open daily May–Sept, weekends Oct–Apr). Should the *rifugio* be full pop down to Fiastra proper, the modest lakeside resort, as follows.

First walk down to the actual village of Trebbio (groceries, bus to Camerino and Bolognola). The name is apparently a reference to the intersection of three roads. Time permitting, detour over the road to the church, a curious

View over Fiastra lake

combination of a Romanesque facade and red brick 20th-century bell tower. Nearby are the meagre ruins of the erstwhile imposing Castrum Fiastrae where people and their livestock would take refuge from barbarian invasions during the turbulent medieval times.

On the main road, turn R along the road past the Casa del Parco. A lane soon breaks off R, leading down through woods to the road bridge across the end of Lago di Fiastrone and up to

It's worth staying an extra day to explore the wonderful Lame Rosse (Walk 2) and Gole del Fiastrone canyon (Walk 1) though this second option necessitates procuring a lift to Monastero.

15mins – Fiastra (651m) ATM, groceries, B&B Osteria al Lago ☎ 0737 52669. The name is believed to derive from a local term for 'river', or Latin for 'valley'. The Fiume Fiastrone was dammed in the 1950s for generating hydroelectric power. By all means join the locals and indulge in a swim in the inviting turquoise waters but limit yourself to the area immediately in front of the modest beach. Do *not* venture out far from the shore as river flow and currents can be treacherous. ◂

STAGE 3

Fiastra to Garulla

Time	7hrs
Distance	25km/15.5 miles
Ascent/descent	1200m/1000m

The initial stretch as far as Pintura del Ragnolo is arguably the least interesting of the whole of the GAS. Immediately afterwards however, having gained a broad crest edged by a string of minor peaks with sheer eastern cliffs that drop precipitously to the Piceno plain, far-reaching views stretching to the Adriatic coast are enjoyed. Subsequently the northernmost Sibillini are constantly on view, an exciting prospect that includes Pizzo Tre Vescovi and Monte Priora. Beyond the modest ski resort of Pintura di Bolognola the GAS begins its descent along the range's eastern flanks touching on the first of a string of attractive villages. All in all it is remarkably tiring due to the countless ups and downs, but naturally immensely rewarding.

Note: unlike the original plan as shown on maps, the GAS does not go to Monastero as it offers no facilities. The signs on the first section still give Monastero as the destination, which is fine as far as the junction highlighted in the description below. This also means that the stage is overly long so by all means make an overnight stop at either Pintura di Bolognola or Bolognola itself.

From **Fiastra** (651m) and its lake go S along the road signposted for Bolognola and lined with scented lime trees, but after 5mins turn L (NE). Albergo Sasso Bianco is soon passed (☎ 0737 52129 www.albergosasso bianco.com) and a lane carries on to the chapel **Madonna del Sasso Bianco** (1006m). Light woodland covers these gentle hills, home to timid roe deer. Where the route bears E in Valle Terra Nera waymarks are few and far between, and you need to part ways with

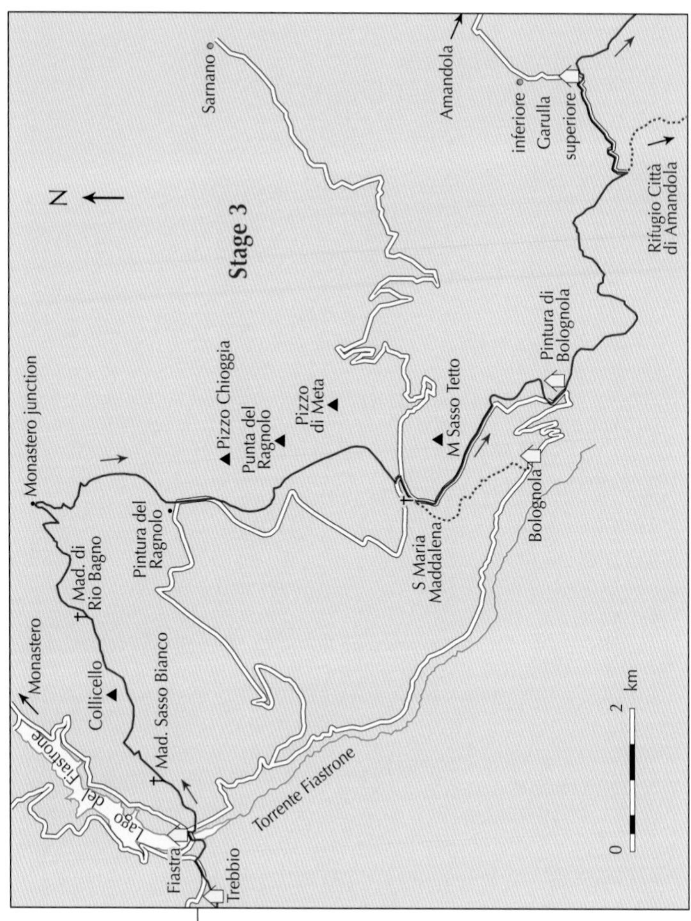

the valley floor and climb up towards Collicella and a spring at 1026m, amidst juniper and wild rose shrubs. The next useful landmark is the tiny chapel of **Madonna di Rio Bagno** (922m). Thereafter the path (N) flanks white diagonal rock strata, climbing once again to a 4WD track. High above fields, the Cerro (1027m) knoll is crossed and a path soon takes over NE in descent through atmospheric woodland of holm oak and holly, well frequented by wild boar, judging from the muddy criss-cross tracks. Not far on you emerge at a lane and

2hrs 30mins – Monastero junction (967m). Ignore the signs that point L for Monastero.

Turn R with a lovely outlook facing E over rolling cultivated hills and woodland. Soon a steep path ascends through beech to join a broad gravel track. This leads S onto the vast, elevated grassy plateau of

50mins – Pintura del Ragnolo (1305m), a favourite with roaming mushroom hunters, also a nature reserve, blessed with a fabulous spread of spring flowers starring exquisite wild orchids. Incongruous steep-gabled chalets are dotted here and there for the enjoyment of cross-country ski lovers, when there are sufficient winter snow falls.

View to the Piceno plain beyond Pizzo di Meta

A minor road is joined due S (Bolognola direction) but not far on, the GAS forks L to climb diagonally along the western side of triangular Pizzo Chioggia. A windswept tundra-like landscape is traversed, marvellously open and with unhindered views E. Beyond the abrupt dizzy edge of this upland, the rolling Piceno hills spread towards the Adriatic coast a mere 50km away. Modest crags Punta del Ragnolo then Pizzo di Meta are passed, both brilliant panoramic points (worth a detour). In the other direction interesting Sibillini peaks appear SW, the line-up takes in Monte Castel Manardo SSE, Monte Priora S and Monte Rotondo SSW, while close at hand, crowned with ski lifts and antennas, is Monte Sasso Tetto.

The tarmac is reached at 1457m and you turn L in the direction of Bolognola as the road curves around Monte Sasso Tetto for 2.5km.

Short cut to Bolognola (40mins)

If you plan to sleep at Bolognola, this handy short cut saves the ensuing stretch on monotonous asphalt. Only metres along the road from the 1457m point, break off R at the small chapel of **Santa Maria Maddalena**. A clear path descends SW to a signed fork at 1314m. Here you turn L – for 'Bolognola alta' – slotting into the upper branch of the *Sentiero Natura* marked by red/white stripes with a green 'N' (see Walk 4). This descends diagonally past the enclosure for the Apennine chamois reintroduced in 2006. In no time you're in **Bolognola** (1061m). Turn L for the hotel (see below), bus stop and groceries.

At a bend the GAS breaks off L briefly uphill for a path over wooded Monte Valvasetto before dropping to

2hrs 10mins – Pintura di Bolognola (1312m), comprising a cluster of chalets, ski lifts, Albergo La Capanna (☎ 0737 520134 www.capannabolognola.it) and B&B Cristina e Laura (who arrange for dinner, ☎ 0737 520136). It is also feasible to go down to Bolognola (3km away) where there are groceries and a bus via Fiastra to Camerino if needed.

Friendly old-style Hotel Bucaneve (☎ 0737 520131) guarantees a shuttle service to and from Pintura for its guests, and also feeds them royally. On foot to Bolognola allow 30mins: cut down the slopes, dodging the avalanche barriers, then take the road.

At the rear of Albergo la Capanna follow the gravel lane that heads ESE into beech woods. Minor ups and downs characterise the ensuing winding stretch, with some lovely views opening up to the Piceno plains as you head E. Towering above (S) are the vast bare ridges of Monte Castel Manardo succeeded by Monte Amandola further around. About 1hr from Pintura, near park signs denoting the border of the protected area, the GAS turns suddenly L (N).

Variant via Rifugio Città di Amandola (40mins)
This variant takes you on an alternative route which cuts out the first part of Stage 4. It stays slightly higher than the GAS and is useful if you wish to explore Monte Amandola on Walk 5. Stay on the lane as it continues SE to a fork then turn R (S) on the gravel road for the final 2km to Campolungo and **Rifugio Città di Amandola (1185m).** Mobile ☎ 347 1921635, sleeps 8, open July–Aug + weekends all year round, www.rifugiocittadiamandola.com. Bright establishment run by a keen young couple who do freshly baked cakes and mouth-watering lasagne. The only drawback is the possible limited use of the shower. The place was originally built as a cable-car station which explains the cavernous interior; fortunately for nature lovers the ski-lift project came to nothing!

To Capovalle (45mins)
In common with Walk 5, leave the hut on path n.225/MTB4, heading downhill S, overlooking the deep gash of Valle dell'Ambro. At a shoulder in an area used by woodcutters the route veers briefly R (SW) to join a lane – turn L here on path MTB4 for **Capovalle** (774m) where you pick up the main GAS route – see Stage 4.

The brand new rifugio at Garulla

Keep a close watch on waymarks as the faint path descends through woods alive with squirrels. The odd field with grazing sheep is touched on. At a minor asphalt road (from Campolongo and Rifugio Città di Amandola) you keep L. Not far down, a path threads through the houses belonging the sleepy farming hamlet of

1hr 30mins – Garulla superiore (870m). Only minutes down the road is brand new Rifugio Garulla (☎ 338 6182494 www.rifugiogarulla.it), a tastefully designed modern structure with all mod cons. Sleeps 36, open Apr–Oct + weekends.

STAGE 4

Garulla to Rubbiano

Time	3hrs 30mins
Distance	10.4km/6.5 miles
Ascent/descent	480m/550m

Today you proceed along the lovely eastern flanks of the Sibillini. En route are wonderful views across rolling cultivated hills dotted with historic fortified townships, beyond which is the Adriatic coast. The GAS cuts across two notable deep river valleys, the Ambro and the Tenna, whose flows originate in mountain springs. The Valle dell'Ambro boasts a church on a hallowed spot where a shepherdess regained the power of speech thanks to an apparition of the Madonna. For the Marche region this sanctuary is second only to world-famous Loreto in terms of popularity. The upper valley narrows to a tremendous ravine, but dangerous rock falls have unfortunately closed it to visitors. The Tenna valley on the other hand is both accessible and justifiably popular as the Gole dell'Infernaccio canyon is here, a must-see detour from Rubbiano, explained at the relevant spot below as well as Walk 9.

Note: should the *rifugio* at Rubbiano not be open, continue on to Isola San Biagio (50mins further on, Stage 5) where there's a good choice of lodgings.

From the *rifugio* at **Garulla** (870m) the GAS leads off through deciduous woodland and fields. Views E take in rolling cultivated hills dotted with villages. Past clay slopes the path dips to the solitary 11th-century **Abbazia di San Salvatore** (770m) also known as Vincenzo e Anastasio. A lane climbs to the deserted hamlet of **Casalicchio** (860m) with a drinking fountain and a good outlook to Monte Amandola WSW where you may be lucky to spot an eagle. The Gran Sasso group and the famous Corno Grande will hopefully also be visible S. Now, sharp L, the way drops through woodland and across a field to a lane at the foot of the curious, grey argillaceous outcrop

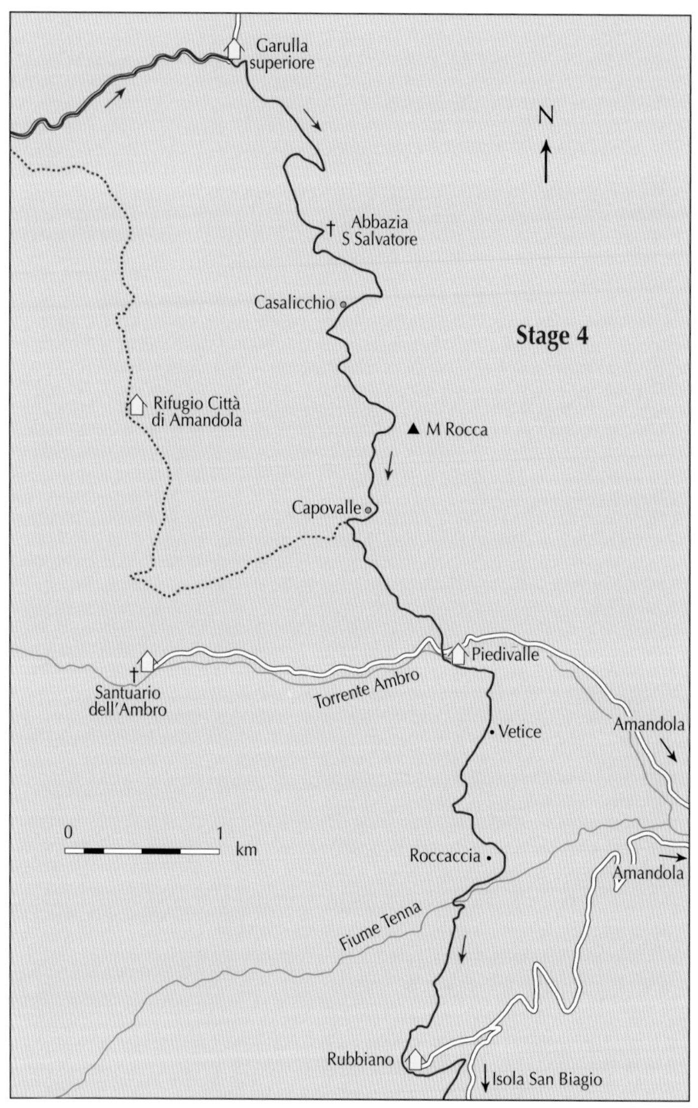
Garulla
superiore
N
Abbazia
S Salvatore
Casalicchio
Stage 4
Rifugio Città
di Amandola
M Rocca
Capovalle
Piedivalle
Santuario
dell'Ambro
Torrente Ambro
Vetice
Amandola
0
1
km
Roccaccia
Amandola
Fiume Tenna
Rubbiano
Isola San Biagio

Monte Priora and Monte Sibilla can be admired during Stage 4

Monte Rocca, remarkably similar to giant elephants' toes. Views are now dominated by soaring Monte Sibilla and Monte Priora SW. It's not far to the farming village of **Capovalle** (774m) in a lovely position for appreciating the Valle dell'Ambro, and where the variant via Rifugio Città di Amandola rejoins the GAS. Take care not to miss the waymarks sharp L at the last house, and follow signs carefully down through woodland and fields to

2hrs – Piedivalle (604m). A peaceful rural village crawling with cats. On the roadside is friendly B&B Da Maria ☎ 0736 859113. Alternative accommodation and meals can be found 2km W along the road at the Santuario dell'Ambro – Albergo Da Peppinè ☎ 0736 859171.

Strange as it may seem, walkers on the GAS now need to open the sliding gate of Da Maria to reach Torrente Ambro and the footbridge. ▸ A clear path climbs the opposite bank through damp woods to **Vetice** (690m) whence an asphalted road. Paths then lead through rural

Note: the footbridge may be impassable after heavy rain if the watercourse is swollen

Hamlet of Rubbiano

properties – a number of gates need closing after you. At the bottom of a field is the attractive tower and renovated **Roccaccia**, and soon afterwards you're down on the banks of Fiume Tenna which flows out of the spectacular Gole dell'Infernaccio upstream (see Walk 9). Amidst the scent of aromatic herbs a lovely stretch of path SW follows the stream touching on crumbly red rock strata. Upstream loom Il Pizzo and Monte Sibilla on opposite sides of the valley. A bridge crosses to the S bank for a stiff but scenic climb through woods and fields to tranquil

1hr 30mins – Rubbiano (805m). Clusters of houses scattered over the hillsides on the lower slopes of Monte Zampa, and inhabited by well-fed chickens. B&B Ca' de la Rossa (☎ 333 8412523 www.bbcadelarossa sibillini.jimdo.com) is a convenient substitute for the still-unopened rifugio.

A minor road passes through the higher part of the village leading W into the Gole dell'Infernaccio – see Walk 9 for the memorable canyon walk.

STAGE 5

Rubbiano to Colle di Montegallo

Time	4hrs
Distance	13.5km/8.4 miles
Ascent/descent	750m/500m

Characterised by the occasional rural hamlet and inspiring non-stop vistas, most of today is spent wandering through beautiful, quiet woodland beneath the eastern flanks of landmark Monte Sibilla, which gave its name to the whole chain. That exciting ridge and summit can be explored by making a detour just after Isola San Biagio – see below. What's more, the GAS encounters the Aso, another deep-running valley cut out of these eastern mountainsides by a watercourse. An original and extremely worthwhile variant is to proceed up the road to Foce, then the stiff path via Lago di Pilato, making a spectacular traverse to Forca di Presta (see Walk 15 and Stage 6). This can also be converted into a route to Castelluccio (see Stage 6 and Walk 16).

From the minor road through **Rubbiano** (805m) the GAS takes a waymarked lane E that climbs to a corner looking over to fortified Mortefortino. A delightful level stretch ensues, mostly S via lanes and fields on the lower reaches of Monte Zampa, an outlier of Monte Sibilla.

About 40mins from Rubbiano the road and an abandoned quarry are reached.

Only minutes L down the road (above Colle Regnone) is friendly family-run Agriturismo Le Castellare ☎ 0736 856270 www.lecastellare.it with spotless accommodation and never-ending meals with home-grown ingredients.

Turn R along the tarmac to the nearby rural settlement of

50mins – Isola San Biagio (932m). Accommodation at Agriturismo Le Fate ☎ 0736 856239 or Agriturismo Le Oreadi ☎ 0736 856251 www.leoreadi.com.

Stick to the road for a further 15mins to where a lane breaks off R uphill for Rifugio Sibilla which you ignore (see Walk 10 for the Monte Sibilla circuit). The attractive town of Montemonaco stands SE with its landmark towers. Very soon the GAS leaves the tarmac, turning R (S) next to a house at **Collina**. With views SSW to Monte Banditello and Vettore a lovely lane lined with hedgerows descends easily into pretty woods and the hamlet of **Tofe** (747m). This lies in the valley of the River Aso, which ends up dammed in Lago di Gerosa. Of greater interest to walkers is the fact that 5km W upstream is the village of Foce and a path for Lago di Pilato (see Walk 15). There is also hotel accommodation 1.5km W at Rocca (Albergo Guerrin Meschino ☎ 0736 856218 www.guerrinmeschino.com) as well as the occasional bus to Montemonaco and beyond.

Turn L along the road past the old church of S. Maria in Casalicchio. Then, at nearby **Pignotti** (737m) branch R past the restaurant Locanda La Trota which, true to its name, serves trout. Once over the river the GAS turns R as a path for a climb through lovely chestnut woods and terraced fields. It emerges on grassy

Agriturismo Le Castellare

slopes dotted with oak trees to views taking in the Aso and Lago di Gerosa E, without forgetting Monte Sibilla behind you now NW, and the exciting line-up ahead WSW with Cima della Prata and the succession to Monte Vettore. The next landmark is

1hr 40mins – Altino (1035m) an enchanting hamlet with the usual drinking fountain and tiny church, along with summer-only accommodation (Residence Villaggio Turistico Altino ☎ 338 1698492 www.altinosibillini.it).

A lane continues due S down dry hillsides bathed in the scent of aromatic thyme and other herbs before chestnut woods are reached. A number of streams are crossed and the vegetation turns to divine beech trees. There is widespread evidence of wild boar here as the animals come in to scratch greedily around in search of edible nuts. At a rise, walkers are treated to a dramatic look at Monte Vettore, especially sheer and dominating from this angle. The GAS descends to a fountain (Sorgente Santa 1159m, where a 10min return detour is recommended to the ancient 8th-century church of **S. Maria del Pantano**, which translates roughly as Our Lady of the Bog).

Beautiful beech woods

Soon you fork L (SSW) for

1hr 30mins – Colle di Montegallo (1015m). Rifugio Sottovento (☎ 0736 806310 www.rifugiocollesibillini.it), sleeps 24, has an excellent reputation for hospitality. (Should you need groceries or buses, continue another 1hr to Balzo – see the detour in Stage 6 below.)

This quiet village occupies a lovely panoramic position on the edge of a funnel-shaped valley head, at the foot of the Monte Vettore–Torrone ridge. Fed by copious springs, a good three watercourses run down these slopes, gouging out deep ruts, perfect for channelling the winter snow. In fact a particularly destructive avalanche hit in 1934, wiping out the village of Casale, wisely reconstructed in a safer, higher position as Casale Nuovo a short way above Colle itself.

STAGE 6

Colle di Montegallo to Colle le Cese

Time	5hrs 15mins
Distance	18.5km/11.5 miles
Ascent/descent	820m/350m

Today a good part of the GAS runs above the tree line, making sun protection essential.

This is the final day of the GAS on the eastern side of the Sibillini, as after the key road pass at Forca di Presta it gains the broad crests surmounting the vast Piano Grande di Castelluccio. Here time out for a number of worthwhile detours is urged – namely the ascent of the Sibillini's highest peak, Monte Vettore, as well as a detour across the plateau to the iconic village of Castelluccio. Otherwise the GAS continues by way of ridges, with marvellous vast outlooks, concluding at a quiet low-key winter ski zone where a choice of accommodation is on offer.

From **Colle di Montegallo** (1015m) head downhill SE by way of the lovely old paved track through atmospheric woodland to the church of **Santa Croce** (922m, 10mins).

Detour to Balzo (50mins)

If needs be, turn L (due E) on the signed path that follows a stream to an old mill and road bridge, after which a short stretch of tarmac leads up to the friendly village of **Balzo** (886m). Groceries, buses to Ascoli Piceno and good value accommodation and meals are available at Villa Emma (☎ 0736 807004 www.villaemmabandb.it) or B&B Lo Spuntino ☎ 0736 806467 www.casavacanzelospuntino.it, who organise transport to and from Colle with a little advance warning.

Turn R along the asphalt, past the little graveyard, for the lane through a picnic area. Two streams are soon crossed and you follow signs for Colleluce, a minuscule

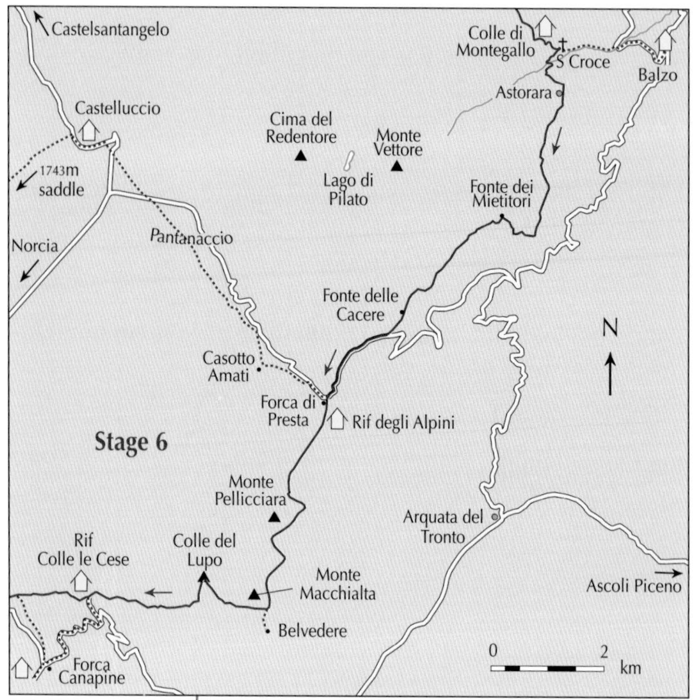

hamlet. Then it's L and through to the road at **Astorara** (1008m) where the GAS turns R, past a church, for a stony track climbing steadily S through open fields. The magnificent Pizzo outcrop on Monte Vettore soars up ahead W. A wider lane is joined for Colle Pisciano (1270m), with grey argillaceous rock slabs underfoot and lovely outlooks in all directions. The path leads through beautiful beech and conifer woods and across bleached white scree flows reminiscent of the Italian Dolomites. A vast curve W leads around the base of Monte Pianello della Macchia to **Fonte dei Mietitori**, once an important spring for the itinerant reapers who would tread this Sentiero dei Mietitori on their peregrinations in search of work.

The Monte Vettore ridge

The next useful landmark is the **Fonte delle Cacere** before you climb out onto open pasture and soon join the road that climbs from Arquata del Tronto. Turn R (SW) for the final 30mins via Sasso Tagliato 'cut rock' to

3hrs 15mins – Forca di Presta (1534m). The place name is believed to derive from either *prestito* for 'loan', referring to ancient land leasing practices, or possibly from *praesto* for 'a place high up'.

Variant to Castelluccio (2hrs)

This straightforward route cuts across the Piano Grande on cart tracks. From Forca di Presta walk NW down the road past a spring and drinking troughs to where a clear path (n.557) forks L and descends below the level of the road past a surviving tongue of beech woodland. Close to ruined **Casotto Amati** (1373m) an unnumbered lane turns N, parallel to the road, and through fields planted with the area's famous lentils. Skirting the base of La Rotonda, a favourite launching pad for hang gliders, it heads across the vast altopiano. At a 1296m fork in an area known as the Pantanaccio (ghastly bog!) take the L branch which crosses the road and leads to the foot of the knoll with Castelluccio. Here a track shortcuts the road for the short climb to the village of **Castelluccio** (1452m).

Accommodation possibilities include comfortable rooms and inspirational meals at the Taverna Castelluccio (☎ 0743 821158 or 0743 821100 www.tavernacastelluccio.it) and Locanda dè Senari (☎ 0743 821205 www.agriturismosenari.it) amongst others.

Return to the GAS (1hr 30mins)

From **Castelluccio** (1452m) take the dirt track that breaks off alongside Albergo Sibilla heading SW below Monte Veletta then Coste le Prata. With vast views across Piano Grande, it swings below Poggio di Croce before turning due W as a path to rejoin the GAS at the **1743m saddle** in Stage 7.

With fleeting views over the vast expanse of Piano Grande and even Castelluccio on its perch, only a short walk away is friendly old-style **Rifugio degli Alpini** at 1574m (☎ 0736 809278, www.rifugiomontisibillini.it, sleeps

Monte Vettore from the Belvedere

34, open mid-June to mid-Sept + many weekends) where meals are memorable and the atmosphere great fun. Full-scale refurbishment is on the drawing board. The hut is a perfect base for exploring Monte Vettore (Walk 17).

Continue S in slight ascent on the broad gravel track across bare pastureland skirting Monte Pellicciara. Not far on where the track bears W, by all means take the short detour along a wooden walkway to a **Belvedere** where helpful panoramic photo panels identify mountain ranges near and far. Standing out dramatically to the SE is Pizzo del Selva in the Monti della Laga range while in the distant E is the light-coloured massif Monte dei Fiori.

Proceed due W on the wide track beneath Monte Macchialta, and where it rounds a corner watch out for a faintly marked path R (NW) uphill over karstic terrain. A modest rise is reached with stunning views over the Piano Grande altopiano with the hilltop settlement of Castelluccio, not to mention the central Sibillini peaks.

At **Colle del Lupo** (1610m, 'col of the wolf') turn L (SSW) onto a lane back into beech woods, then out onto broad scenic crests, the last leg W to the broad saddle and modest ski area of

2hrs – Colle le Cese (1484m). Rifugio di Colle le Cese (☎ 0736 808102 www.rifugiocollelecese.it), sleeps 37. A hotel rather than a walkers' refuge this place offers comfortable rooms with en suites. Dinner will hopefully include *lasagne con funghi e piselli selvaggi* (baked pasta with mushrooms and native peas). Mini-bus taxi service available.

Another option can be found at nearby Forca Canapine, from where you can slot back into the GAS the following morning without backtracking. Otherwise there's bustling Rifugio Perugia, 1hr away on the official GAS route – see Stage 7.

Detour to Forca Canapine (30mins)

Follow the tarmac L (S) downhill to a fork and turn R along the road past small hotels to the pass **Forca Canapine** (1541m). Here stands friendly family-run Rifugio Genziana, formerly known as Rifugio Vittorio Ratti (☎ 0743 828623, sleeps 20, open June–Oct).

Return to the GAS (10mins)

To return to the main route, take the minor road NW signed for Rifugio Monti del Sole (no accommodation), a short stroll away at 1574m, a transit point for Stage 7.

STAGE 7

Colle le Cese to Campi Vecchio

Time	6hrs
Distance	20km/12.4 miles
Ascent/descent	450m/1100m

Today commences with magnificent vistas over to the peaks of Cima del Redentore and its neighbours. The broad ridges that form the western lip of the Piano Grande are followed in succession, offering bird's-eye views of the walled Umbrian town of Norcia. A long descent takes walkers to delightful pastoral Valle del Campiano where bed and board can be had in an exceptionally pretty hamlet.

Note: this is a long stage (shortened marginally by overnighting at Rifugio Perugia); moreover clear visibility is essential for the faint path on the latter section as landmarks are lacking. Should low cloud or adverse conditions look imminent be prepared to detour to Castelluccio from the 1743m saddle.

From **Colle le Cese** (1484m) the GAS heads W along a wooded ridge that affords lovely views over Pian Piccolo taking in the Redentore peak. Old ski lifts are encountered en route. Follow pole markers carefully through the web of paths and after about 20mins you reach a car park and snack bar Rifugio Monti del Sole (1574m), incorrectly placed on some maps. The variant from Forca Canapine joins up here.

The path cuts around the base of modest Monte Cappelletta offering lovely views over the Umbrian hills and the extensive patchwork fields of the Piano di Santa Scolastica, a subsided valley named in honour of the twin sister of Saint Benedict from Norcia. The road is crossed in the vicinity of

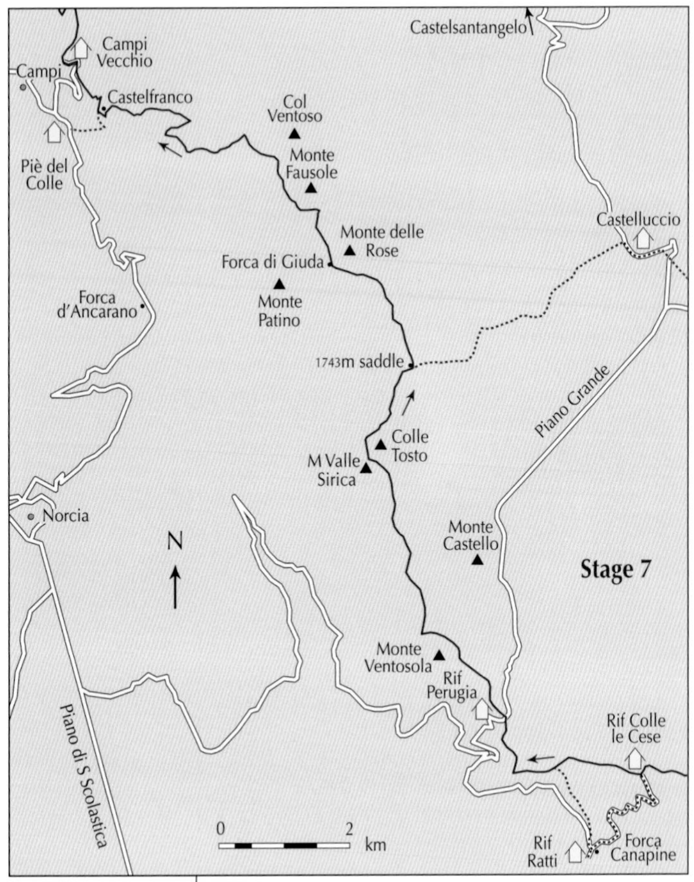

1hr – Rifugio Perugia (1492m). (☎ 0743 82301, sleeps 38, always open, www.rifugioperugia.it), well-run establishment popular with hang-gliders and other airborne enthusiasts.

Proceed NNW on a broad white stony track across the vast slopes of Costa Precino, which act as launching

Piano di S Scolastica

pads for the daring fliers. They glide over the Piano Grande, clearly visible from here with its curious web-like system of the Mergani, natural drainage culminating in the sink hole. After a saddle beneath Monte Ventosola you swing R for a long linear traverse dominated by the perfect cone of Monte Castello, at whose foot extend grazing grounds for horses and sheep. At the far end of this traverse and a series of watering troughs (le Tre Fonti – though there only seem to be two), is a short diagonal climb to a 1684m saddle between Monte Valle Sirica and Colle Tosto for lovely views down to the renowned walled town of Norcia.

Heading due N once more, you coast easily enjoying views all around to

1hr 45mins – 1743m saddle, where a handy path forks R (E) for Castelluccio (see Walk 18); the variant from Forca di Presta joins up here.

Keeping an eye out for red/white paint splashes on rocks and the odd marker pole, continue NW amidst confusing criss-crossing tracks left by generations of grazing livestock. Heading towards the gentle round of Monte delle Rose, the path passes at its foot to

30mins – Forca di Giuda (1794m) the highest point reached on the GAS! Also the turn-off for the straightforward half-hour walk to the top of panoramic 1883m Monte Patino, with its lookout extraordinaire over Norcia – see Walk 14.

Descending from Forca di Giuda

Now it's N cutting across steep grassy inclines (ignore the fork in descent L) to a last panoramic knoll before the descent finally commences below Monte Fausole. A beech copse precedes drinking troughs at

1645m on the lower slopes of Col Ventoso, and here you bear diagonally L (NW). Follow the map carefully on this stretch as the path as such disappears regularly. You bear W to cross a rocky outcrop, then a clearer path enters beech woods, followed by a scree traverse.

Pastoral Valle del Campiano opens up below, its rural settlements dotted along a poplar-lined valley floor. On Costa Cognola, concentrations of juniper bushes then thick beech woodland accompany walkers into a minor valley. It's not far to Valle delle Grotte, a marvellous limestone ravine smothered with Mediterranean maquis vegetation such as holm oak, scented broom and savory herb. The GAS emerges from the valley close to the ruins of **Castelfranco** which dates back to the 15th century. A little further it joins a lane – the GAS turns R. ▶

The L branch leads to the valley floor, a feasible exit via Piè del Colle.

Castelfranco above Capo del Colle

Exit to Piè del Colle (20mins)
A short stroll downhill is Capo del Colle and a beautifully frescoed church. Continue past a drinking fountain to the main road at **Piè del Colle** (752m). Turn L for buses to Norcia and B&B L'Asino che ride (the laughing donkey! ☎ 0743 820051 or mobile 320 1723752, open April to mid-Oct, www.bbnorcia.it). A family-run pizzeria/restaurant is only minutes away. Not to be confused with nearby Piedivalle, the village is also spelt Piedicolle and sometimes referred to as Ancarano. The closest grocery shop can be found 2km away at Campi.

Today's 30min concluding leg goes N, on the upper edge of fields and light woodland, before joining the road to enter the arched portal into the enchanting village of

2hrs 45mins – Campi Vecchio (907m) ie 'old Campi' composed of beautifully restored light stone houses and the porticoed church of San Andrea. On the far edge of the village are the renovated premises of Rifugio Campi Alto (☎ 0743 820051 or mobile 320 1723752, sleeps 25, open Easter, June–Sept + weekends www.rifugiosibillini.it).

STAGE 8

Campi Vecchio to Visso

Time	3hrs
Distance	10km/6.2 miles
Ascent/descent	350m/600m

A great contrast to yesterday's ridges and wide vistas, in this relaxing stage you climb away from the farming idyll of Valle del Campiano to follow the quiet wooded Valle di Visso, alive with wildlife. Traces of hare, porcupine and boar abound. An especially elongated valley, it leads N to return to the start point of Visso, crowned with old castles.

From **Campi Vecchio** (907m) the path heads into the lightly wooded Val Majore and along the route of an old aqueduct, to the poignant ruins of the church

Castle above Visso

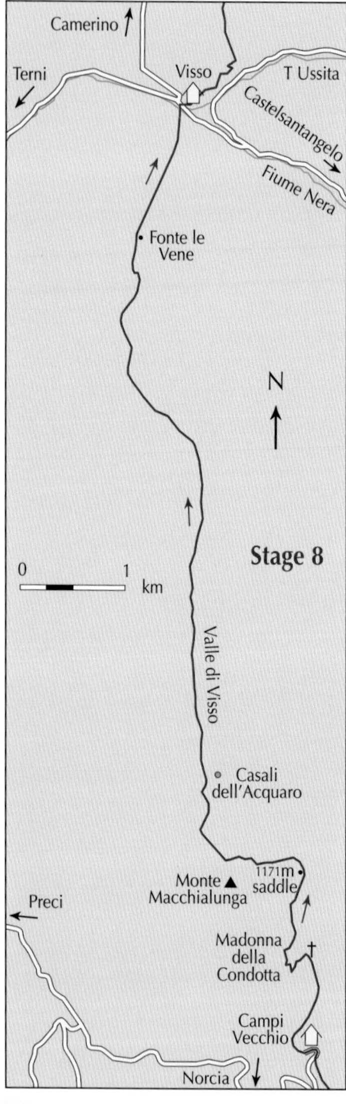

Madonna del Condotto (874m), (our lady of the pipeline), erected at a strategic spring on an old route linking Campi with Castelsantangelo sul Nera. Sadly, little is left of the church's 15th-century frescoes. Here you need to fork L for a zigzagging plod uphill amidst Mediterranean plants such as aromatic herbs and holm oak. A **1171m saddle** between Monte Macchialunga and Monticello is reached, then soon afterwards a good lane leads you L (W) in slight ascent to a bare 1231m knoll where the GAS turns valleywards towards a pocket of cultivated fields and

1hr 20mins – Casali dell'Acquaro (1130m), a scatter of farm buildings.

Make sure you keep on the L (W) side of the hollow. Now it's due N in almost imperceptible descent via peaceful Valle di Visso, once an important communications artery between Visso and Norcia. There's a good chance of meeting woodcutters, who use makeshift metal chutes to transport tree trunks effortlessly. Pink striated rock is often underfoot. The next useful landmark is a small farmhouse and spring, **Fonte Le Vene**. Now the valley opens up and you're treated to views of an old castle with towers and fortified walls snaking down the hillside over Visso. A little further the lane is surfaced, and you're led straight across a road and via a magnificent decorated stone arch into the township of

Visso's main square

1hr 40mins – Visso (685m). As you reach the stone wall containing the river, either turn L for the park HQ to complete the circuit, or go R and into town, where the conclusion of the trek can be suitably celebrated!

See the Introduction and the GAS preface for details of access to/from Visso, as well as accommodation information.

WALK 1

Valle del Fiastrone

Walking time	2hrs 45mins
Difficulty	Grade 2
Ascent/descent	230m/230m
Distance	8.4km/5.2 miles
Start/Finish	Monastero cemetery
Access	Monastero is a short scenic drive NE of Fiastra, or W inland from Sarnano. Leave the main road and turn downhill (N) past the old monastery to the cemetery, where there is parking.

An absolutely delightful walk with great historical and natural interest, as it visits first cliffside caves once inhabited by hermit monks, then a wondrous canyon. This is the eastern section of the Valle del Fiastrone. The river rises in the valley above Bolognola and swings towards

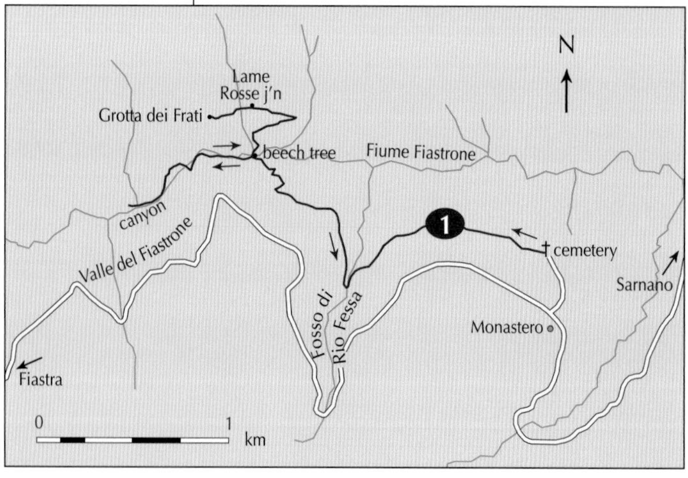

Grotta dei Frati

WALK

From the **Monastero cemetery** (658m) follow the signs for Valle del Fiastrone and Grotta dei Frati along a pretty lane W. It descends easily into holm oak woods, with marvellously promising views over the thickly wooded valley, where gashes of onion-layered red rock appear on the cliffs. The path narrows, but is always clear and well marked with red paint splashes on tree trunks. It crosses the Fosso di Rio Fessa then becomes fairly steep during the descent to the valley floor. Here is a key junction, recognisable by a huge **beech tree** (482m, 40mins) plastered with signs and numbers (none of which correspond to the maps!). Turn R and cross the stream for the zigzagging climb, ignoring forks (such as the link with Lame Rosse and Walk 2). A final uphill surge is followed by a level bit W along a broad rock ledge with wooden railing beneath towering limestone cliffs. Jungle-like vegetation surrounds the panoramic site of atmospheric **Grotta dei Frati** (615m, 20mins), and you can see down to the canyon. Do wander inside as far as possible to

Entering the Fiastrone canyon

see the cistern and altar, though innermost passages are partially obstructed by rockfalls and collapsed ceilings.

Return to the **beech tree** junction (482m, 15mins) and turn R (W) this time. It's not far along to the first of many river fords – it's a matter of stepping stones or sandals. The dramatic yawning aperture of the Valle del Fiastrone river **canyon** (505m, 20mins) is soon reached. Continue at will along the magical gorge, dwarfed by cliffs tinged pink-red, your feet cooled by the river water. Cascades trickle down the flanks through drapes of creepers and moss.

Afterwards return to the **beech tree** junction (482m, 20mins) and go R for the climb back uphill. En route are marvellous views E where the Fiume Fiastrone reaches the ample plains, and the Sibillini mountains come to a surprisingly abrupt halt. Keep on to the car park at **Monastero cemetery** (658m, 50mins).

Fiastra: B&B Osteria al Lago ☎ 0737 52669
Trebbio: Rifugio di Trebbio ☎ 0737 527027 or mob 333 6733300, www.rifugioditribbio.com, sleeps 18, open daily May–Sept, weekends Oct–Apr.

WALK 2

Lago del Fiastrone and the Lame Rosse

Walking time	4hrs 15mins
Difficulty	Grade 1–2
Ascent/descent	400m/400m
Distance	15km/9.3 miles
Start/Finish	Fiastra
Access	Fiastra is connected by year-round bus from Camerino. By road it can be reached from many directions, including Sarnano in the east. If time is tight, park at the dam and begin the walk there, saving 2hrs.

Immersed in thick green woodland, an amazing slice of red-pink crumbly terrain, possibly formed from ancient alluvial deposits, is being eroded by the elements into awe-inspiring cliffs and tottering pinnacles. Lame Rosse means 'red blades'. They're illuminated to perfection in the morning. It's as though you've wandered into a lost corner of the Middle East. Seeing is believing.

Fiastra lakeside path

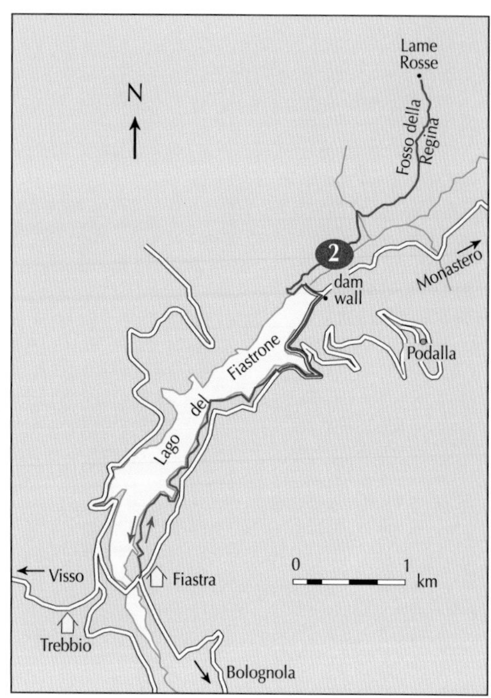

The walk start, Fiastra is believed to refer to a local term for 'river', or Latin for 'valley'. The name is used to refer both to a conglomeration of hamlets and to the lakefront. The body of water came into being in the 1950s when Fiume Fiastrone was dammed for hydro-electric power, submerging the hamlet of San Lorenzo. It entices visitors who bathe in the attractive turquoise waters. Note: swimmers are warned not to venture out too far from the shore as river flow and currents can be treacherous. It is advisable to stick to the beach at Fiastra to cool off.

The initial stretch of this easy walk follows the lake-front as a *sentiero natura* (nature trail). Fishermen and sunbathers make the most of grassy banks and occasional

Fiastra dam

shady trees, and families picnic on the benches. On a hot summer's day set out very early as there is little shade and no drinking water en route.

Note: from the Lame Rosse it is possible to continue on a good path a further 1hr to Grotta dei Frati in Walk 1 (allow 2hrs 30mins for the return trip). However unless you leave a vehicle at Monastero, it's rather too far for a single day.

WALK

Next to Osteria al Lago on the lakefront at **Fiastra** (650m), turn R (N) on the clear path with wooden railing. Close to the water's edge in the company of sweet broom bushes, it passes the camping ground and ducks in and out of a sequence of pretty bays. Standing back from the lake's opposite shore are clay-coloured houses over steep cliffs. At a steep-sided inlet a flight of wooden steps lead up to the Fiastra–Monastero road. Ignore the branch for Podalla and continue to the next bend for a picnic area with an informative panel about the flooding of the valley. The enclosure shelters eye-catching exemplars of wild artichoke. Only minutes

The marvellous Lame Rosse

R (NE) along the tarmac is the **dam wall** (642m, 1hr). Drivers can park along the roadside.

Turn L along the 87m-high, 254m-long wall and through the short tunnel at the end. A path curves up to a signposted junction where you turn R (NE) onto the lower flanks of Monte Fiegni. Below in the deep V-cut is reduced Fiume Fiastrone. A gentle descent through dry holm oak woods leads into wild Val di Nicola, home to roe deer. Ignore the fork for Gole di Fiastrone (see note in Walk 1 preface). The path continues through clearings with rock roses and wild boar scratchings to reach a broad gully, **Fosso della Regina** (775m, 1hr). Turn L (N) in steep ascent. It's easy going over the river of white-pink scree towards the spectacle of the **Lame Rosse** (850m, 15mins).

Return the same way to the **dam wall** (1hr) and on to **Fiastra** (1hr).

See Walk 1 for accommodation.

WALK 3

Cascate dell'Acquasanta

Walking time	4hrs
Difficulty	Grade 2–3
Ascent/descent	50m/50m
Distance	12.4km/7.7 miles
Start/Finish	Bolognola
Access	Year-round buses run from Camerino to Bolognola. Drivers will need the turn-off SE at Fiastra.

An unusual itinerary that penetrates a hidden wild valley – Valle Acquasanta, home to roe deer and timid wild boar – and two impressive waterfalls. It branches S off Valle del Fiastrone, downhill from Bolognola, the walk start. It was thanks to the water pipe put through in

The path to the waterfalls follows the old aqueduct

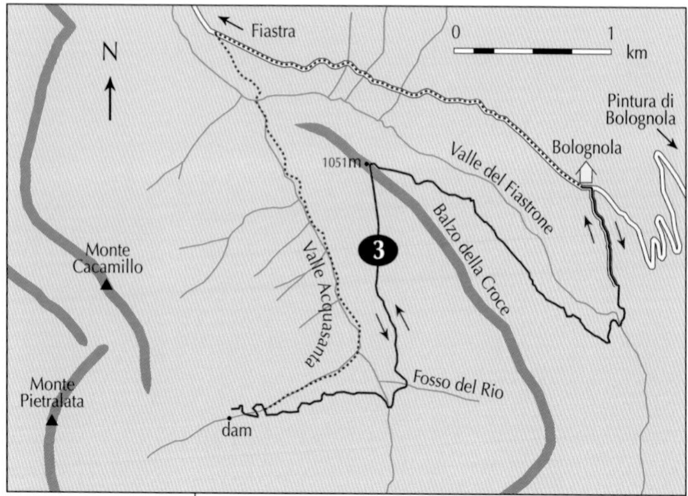

The lovely pathway is on a level virtually the whole way, traversing beautiful beech woods, leading walkers into an out-of-the-way corner of the Sibillini.

the 1920s that the valley became accessible to walkers. Later on, in the mid '80s, a large-scale tunnel was burrowed through the mountain to pipe the water that flows copiously from the 'holy water' (Acquasanta) spring that guarantees the supply for a large community. The path, in fact, follows the old above-ground system of piping, which blends in with the setting. Most visitors do the walk for the cascading waterfalls at its end, clearly at their best in spring but worth a visit at any time. While huge volumes of water should not be expected,hundreds of trickling rivulets covering the rock face make quite a sight. In the vicinity are amazing rock flanks with tight zigzag strata stretching up above your head.

A single warning note: the route deserves the grade 2–3 rating as numerous stretches – at the start and towards the end – entail narrow, moderately exposed lengths of path that necessitate special care. It is unsuitable in wet weather as it can be slippery and potentially dangerous.

Sleepy Bolognola, the walk start, has groceries and a friendly old-style hotel that serves mammoth meals. The walk coincides with the park route E4.

Acquasanta waterfall

WALK

From Hotel Bucaneve at **Bolognola** (Villa di Mezzo, 1061m), just after the whitewashed church turn R (S) on Via Piano signed for the *cascate*. Continue through the picturesque low houses of Villa da Capo to where the road ends. A clear path takes over, n.312, with red/white markings, leading down across two streams before veering R (NW) and narrowing, amidst occasional reminders of the old aqueduct. ◀ Gaps in the vegetation offer lovely views across the valley to the three hamlets that comprise Bolognola.

The going is essentially level through mixed woodland dotted with pretty cyclamens and cutting across incredibly steep mountain flanks.

As the path widens, it runs along the old aqueduct, covered by concrete tiles which resound under the weight of boots. It's like tripping across a piano keyboard, though with only bass notes! The pipeline burrows beneath rock outcrops where necessary. At 1051m **Balzo della Croce** is rounded and the way becomes a broad track heading S into Valle Acquasanta which narrows imperceptibly. Looming ahead SSW is Monte Bambucerta. A workman's hut (for maintenance crews) is passed, then a short stretch of massive metal piping.

After crossing **Fosso del Rio**, a side stream covered with metal grates, the path goes due W into beautiful woods of beech and yew with great slim tall trees, well away now from the pipes which run underground. Quite a few winter avalanches evidently fall here, but path maintenance appears to be pretty good. However, occasional bits can be slippery. One especially tight passage is fitted with a handy chain.

Very soon afterwards is the first of two waterfalls, down rock faces of a million wafer-thin layers. The valley is all but closed in now, while on the opposite side are extraordinarily contorted layers, folded and shifted by unbelievable pressure in an ancient era. After the second waterfall and the entrance to a mountain tunnel for maintenance, is a scramble to the valley floor. Here, surprisingly, you find yourself at the foot of a modest **dam** (1060m, 2hrs) choked with a chaos of fallen trunks.

Beyond, a tantalising magical – but inaccessible – ravine with dizzy walls is glimpsed. To its right ingenious channelling burrows through the cliff face, transporting precious water to a pumping station down the valley.

The way back to **Bolognola** (1061m, 2hrs) is the same as the outward stretch.

Variant return (3hrs 30mins)
Below the dam wall a faint path heads ENE along the floor of **Valle Acquasanta** where it may be obstructed by avalanche debris. It later joins a 4WD track, emerging on the road from Fiastra, 2.5km downhill from Bolognola. While this is attractive as a loop route, be warned that it is much longer and concludes with an inordinately long slog uphill on tarmac.

Hotel Bucaneve ☎ 0737 520131

WALK 4

Bologna Sentiero Natura

Walking time	1hr 30mins
Difficulty	Grade 1
Ascent/descent	250m/250m
Distance	3.4km/2.1 miles
Start/Finish	Bolognola
Access	Year-round buses run from Camerino to Bolognola. Drivers will need the turn-off SE at Fiastra.

In a deep peaceful wooded zone in the northeast Sibillini, this straightforward loop walk gives lovely views over the vast deep Valle del Fiastrone. An official *sentiero natura* (nature trail) of the park, it runs along the flanks of Monte Sasso Tetto, skirting the fenced

Chamois enclosure above Bolognola

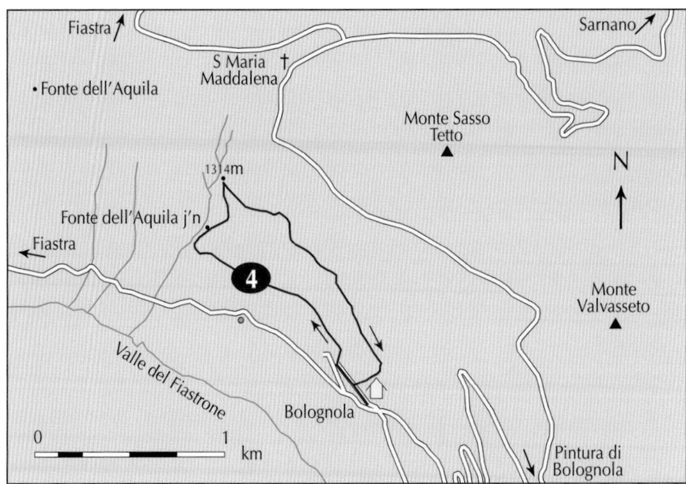

The walk start of Bolognola has an old-style hotel with a traditional restaurant, café and grocery shop.

enclosure set up in 2006 to shelter a pioneer group of Apennine chamois (*Rupicapra pyrenaica ornata*). Two animals were reintroduced to these mountains from the Parco Nazionale della Maiella in Abruzzo. Administered tranquillisers, they were flown in by helicopter to minimise the trauma of travelling. The animals are currently in a state defined as 'semi-liberty' while they settle in. Quiet walkers may strike lucky and spot one grazing close to the path, hopefully with their offspring, born here in 2007.

WALK

From the car park in front of Hotel Bucaneve at **Bolognola** (1061m), turn NW for 'Fonte dell'Aquila'. The route leads along a paved street lined with low stone houses. Soon after the Municipio building is a square with a sculpted Monumento ai caduti, in memory of those who lost their lives in 1930 and 1934 avalanches. Immediately after this turn diagonally R on a lane with red/white and green SN markings. It passes through fields, away from the surfaced road. A clear path takes over, leading gradually uphill to the start of heavy-duty chain-mail anti-avalanche barriers which double in spots as the chamois enclosure. Continuing through holm oak woodland, many views can be enjoyed of the Valle del Fiastrone below, as well as the deep incision of the Valle Acquasanta (S) surmounted by Monte Pietralata. Curving R (NE) a fork is reached: ignore the L branch (NW for renowned spring Fonte dell'Aquila) and turn R for Maddalena. Through a pretty beech copse the path climbs steeply N on an old lane and through a cut rock passage. On open terrain at the upper edge of woodland (**1314m**), the SN forks R (whereas L proceeds for S. Maria Maddalena and a link with the GAS route, Stage 3). Sweeping views SSE take in Monte Castel Manardo and even Monte Priora. Now, through typical dry Mediterranean vegetation, including holm oak and the aromatic curry plant, it's SE in gentle descent past the upper entrance to the chamois area. A steep, gravel-based lane takes over for the rest of the way back to the village. Once down at the houses, turn L back towards the hotel and car park of **Bolognola** (1061m).

Hotel Bucaneve ☎ 0737 520131

WALK 5

Upper Valle dell'Ambro

Walking time	3hrs 45mins
Difficulty	Grade 2 (short stretch Grade 3)
Ascent/descent	690m/690m
Distance	11km/6.8 miles
Start/Finish	Rifugio Città di Amandola
Access	Rifugio Città di Amandola at Campolungo is a 3.5km drive on a good unsurfaced road S from Garulla

Running parallel to the better-known Val Tenna which boasts the Gole dell'Infernaccio (Walk 9), the Valle dell'Ambro is a deep, dark river valley whose middle section is an impassable canyon, the approach to which has unfortunately been closed by dangerous rockfalls. ▶

This walk explores the valley's high northern flanks, with brilliant views to dominant peak Monte Priora and its neighbours.

'Ambro' is believed to derive from the Etruscan term for a leader or priest. On the valley floor is the famous sanctuary Madonna dell'Ambro, second only to Loreto for pilgrim numbers in Italy's Marche region. A church occupies the hallowed spot where the Virgin appeared in a vision to a humble, mute shepherdess, who miraculously regained the power of speech.

The walk start is a *rifugio* set in lovely parkland at Campolungo on the eastern side of Monte Amandola, overlooking a vast sweep of hills stretching to the Adriatic Sea. It is run by an enthusiastic young couple who are great cooks; lasagne comes in generous servings as do the home-made tarts. The place takes on a festive air on the first Sunday in July for the Festa della Montagna – day-long walks, games and naturally, eating. The building is an unusual shape as it was originally intended as a cable-car station for an ambitious ski project, thankfully now relegated to a dusty shelf. The area abounds in wildlife, starting with the clumsy rock partridge. More elegant are the birds of prey that patrol

Rifugio Città di Amandola

the uplands in search of a meal. Roe deer may also be spotted in the woods. Last but not least are memorable displays of wildflowers – wild peonies! lilies! – a delight for summer visitors.

The walk itself is a fine circuit with ongoing panoramas. Beginning with a lovely stretch high over the Valle dell'Ambro, through cool beech woods, it climbs to open grasslands. A single tough stretch is encountered on the approach to Casale Ricci, where an old rockfall and winter avalanches mean a bit of an awkward clamber is necessary. This can be avoided with a lovely if lengthy variant via the Sorgente dell'Ambro – see below and allow at least 1hr 30mins extra.

WALK

Leave **Rifugio Città di Amandola** (1185m) via its drinking fountain. Signs indicate a broad path (n.225/MTB4) which descends S through bushy vegetation and tall

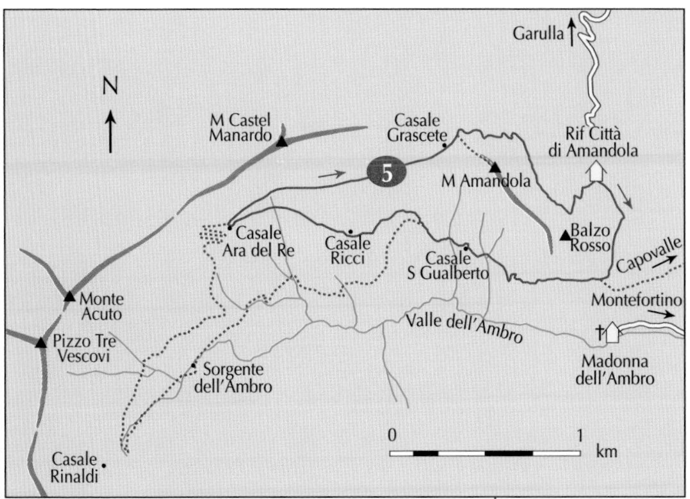

grass where rock partridges may be seen. There are inspiring views to eastern outliers of Monte Priora, then Monte Zampa due S. Below is the deep gash of the Valle dell'Ambro. On a shoulder after 20mins, in an area used by woodcutters, turn R (W) on the clear path leading into shady woods, Le Macchie. This is directly above the well-known sanctuary and ringing bells often echo up the valley. At a nearby junction (1026m) where GAS variant n.MTB4 turns L for Capovalle, you keep R (W). This pretty stretch passes beneath the awesome wall of Balzo Rosso. Ignore the turn-off L for the *santuario* and keep to the old mule track which widens a little.

It's a gentle climb to derelict **Casale San Gualberto** (1243m) and the Fonte del Faggio spring, dry in all likelihood. The outlook is lovely, with a good view of the upper valley and the triangle of Monte Priora. An overgrown stretch with brambles and nettles is followed by cool conifer woods then beech. Keep your eyes peeled for the important fork (10mins from the *casale*) marked by a cairn in the middle of the path and faded n.226 on a tree.

Below the Balzo Rosso

Variant via Sorgente dell'Ambro (2hrs 15mins)
From the turn-off after **Casale San Gualberto** continue W on the clear path via Le Roccacce and the **Sorgente dell'Ambro**. Before Casale Rinaldi is actually reached, fork R on the lane that climbs NE to **Casale Ara del Re**, where the main route is joined.

Turn R on the narrow path, overgrown at times. A messy scree slope soon needs to be traversed – watch your step. Swept by winter avalanches it may be strewn with awkward fallen trees. Over the other side a final climb, concluding with a short zigzag on an old mule track, emerges on a grassy slope, the trees left behind. There is no path as such, but only minutes away WSW over a rise is **Casale Ricci** (1477m) in a marvellously panoramic position. Opposite SW is Monte Priora, while the head of the valley is closed off by Monte Acuto, Pizzo Tre Vescovi and the long blade of Pizzo Berro.

The going becomes easy again on a clear track W to herders' hut **Casale Ara del Re** (2hrs 15mins, 1620m), where the variant joins up. The denomination is curious: it probably means 'the king's altar' and is located directly across the valley from Ara della Regina, the 'queen's altar'.

Fork R (ENE) for the lane beneath Monte Castel Manardo, erstwhile site of a medieval castle. It traverses the stony pasture of Pescolla towards gently sloping Monte Amandola, favourite hunting arena for elegant hawks. Soon after tumble-down **Casale Grascete** (1708m) is a junction.

Monte Amandola (30min detour)
Even before reaching the junction at 1708m by all means cut R (E) across the grassy hillsides pointing your boots in the direction of the cross atop **Monte Amandola** (1706m). On the eastern edge of the Sibillini, it understandably has sweeping views towards the Adriatic coast. To resume the main descent, head back towards the junction to pick up the path.

The gorgeous martagon lily

Clumps of peonies, scented pinks and lilies of both the martagon and orange varieties flourish here.

Even though no path is evident at this point, leave the lane without delay, forking R (E) between 2 hillocks. Not far over the other side you may have to hunt around a little to localise the cairns, after which the way is clear for the lovely traverse SSE down the flank of Monte Amandola. It hosts a remarkable display of wildflowers, sheltered from the prevailing winds. ◂ In the picnic clearing well below stands the *rifugio,* while the rolling hills of the Marche spread towards the Adriatic. Beech copses dot the route which swings NE on the last leg to **Rifugio Città di Amandola** (1hr 30mins, 1185m).

Rifugio Città di Amandola Mobile ☎ 347 1921635 sleeps 8, open July–Aug and weekends year-round exc. Oct. www.rifugiocittadiamandola.com.

WALK 6

Val di Panico and Pizzo Tre Vescovi

Walking time	4hrs 30mins
Difficulty	Grade 2
Ascent/descent	1060m/1060m
Distance	13.5km/8.3 miles
Start/Finish	Casali
Access	The hamlet of Casali is 5km W of Ussita.

A wonderful day loop route that is strenuous, varied and little frequented. A string of wild valleys is traversed en route to a magnificent stretch of scenic crest. The highlight is Pizzo Tre Vescovi, a forbidding sharp-edged triangle that rises to the rear of Forcella del Fargno, but is of surprisingly straightforward access. That said, the final aerial ridge approach may not be to everyone's liking: it is easily avoided thanks to a short cut near unpronounceable Fonte Angagnola (pronounce the 'gn' like 'ny'). A further variation is possible by linking into Walk 7, destination Monte Priora. ▶

Note: the walk is unsuitable during high winds due to the exposed ridge sections.

The outward leg climbs via Val di Panico. Rather then 'panic', or 'pagan' from an ancient temple, or even a cereal crop, the valley may be named after Pan, the divine flautist reputed to have performed here in days long gone by. Even today, shrill and eerie tones waft over the upper valley, usually attributable, however, to wind playing on the old ski lift cables atop Monte Bove Sud SSE.

Dominated by the soaring limestone face of magnificent Monte Bove Nord, the start point, Casali, is a pretty mountain village high above Torrente Ussita in the eponymous valley. It has but a handful of inhabitants, who gather of an afternoon on benches beneath a magnificent ancient chestnut tree, next to the photogenic Romanesque church. A bonus here is Rifugio Casali, a perfect base for visiting the valley. Run by an

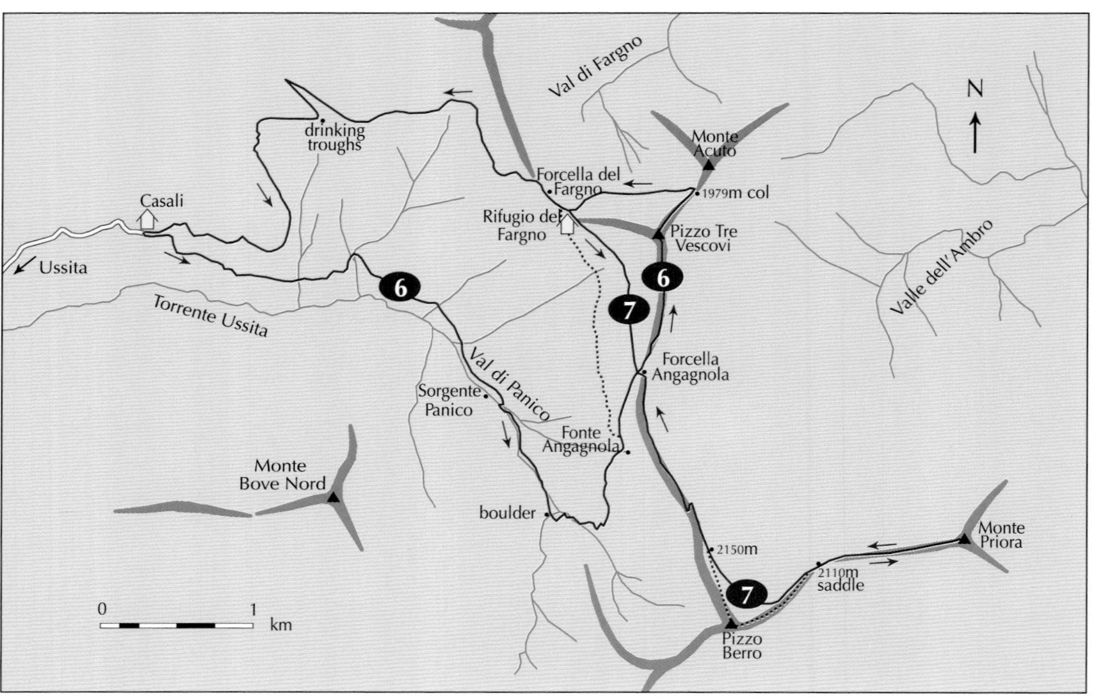
N
Val di Fargno
drinking troughs
Monte Acuto
Forcella del Fargno
1979m col
Casali
Rifugio del Fargno
Pizzo Tre Vescovi
Ussita
6
Valle dell'Ambro
7
Torrente Ussita
Forcella Angagnola
Val di Panico
Sorgente Panico
Fonte Angagnola
Monte Bove Nord
boulder
Monte Priora
2150m
2110m saddle
0
1
km
Pizzo Berro

Below Pizzo Tre Vescovi

affable expert mountaineer it occupies the former school building.

WALK

From the church at **Casali** (1080m) take the gravel road E, alias n.275, which soon becomes closed to unauthorised traffic. With constant inspiring views to awesome Monte Bove Nord and back to the township of Ussita and its castle, this ascends gently SE to where the road curves away R and a red/white path breaks off, continuing SE. This leads past the spring **Sorgente Panico** (50mins, 1346m), mostly channelled through pipes behind an iron gate, though deliciously cool water still trickles down the rock face. Continuing uphill in beautiful Val di Panico, the path zigzags over grassland thick with wild thyme, dog roses and low juniper bushes as well as tracts of scree and bowl-shaped dolina depressions. A useful landmark is the remains of an old hut at a large **boulder** (1550m) at the foot of a massive rock outcrop that divides the valley in two. The clear path

Rifugio del Fargno could be mistaken for a bunker

bears L (E) into a peaceful side valley surmounted by the elongated crest of Pizzo Berro. A wealth of flowers including martagon lilies can be admired. You climb N via a grassy shoulder directly opposite Monte Bove Nord, then just around the corner (1775m) near **Fonte Angagnola**, path n.277 forks L (N) as a short cut to Rifugio del Fargno, handy if the summit crest is not appealing. However for the main route keep up for **Forcella Angagnola** (1hr 30mins, 1924m), a broad saddle on the crest that links Pizzo Berro with Pizzo Tre Vescovi, overlooking the Valle dell'Ambro.

The final climb goes due N. Watch your step and keep to the R side of the grassy ridge to **Pizzo Tre Vescovi** (30mins, 2092m) and its summit cross, named for the former boundaries of three bishoprics. Straight over the other side is the short descent NE to the **1979m col** at the foot of Monte Acuto. Here veer L (W) for the clear if narrow path across dry terrain over the head of Val di Fargno. At windswept **Forcella del Fargno** (40mins, 1811m) you are joined by the dirt roads from Pintura di

Bolognola and Casali. The landmark is the incongruous concrete bunker **Rifugio del Fargno,** singularly unattractive but of great strategic importance. Erected by a group of enthusiasts, it began life as a corrugated sheet iron structure which was blasted far away by strong winds the very first winter, to be followed by a brick building which didn't fare much better. This round concrete affair seems to have done the trick! The location is superb, facing Monte Bove Nord SW, Pizzo Berro SE and close to Monte Rotondo NW.

Take the wide unsurfaced road NW beneath Monte Rotondo (some maps indicate a lower path but it is damnably hard to pinpoint). An enjoyable half an hour along, with views to Monte Cardosa and Monte Torrone over Ussita, at 1737m a clear path, n.278, forks L (SE). It drops to **drinking troughs** (1688m) supplied with deliciously cool water. The vast sweep of Val di Panico headed by Pizzo Berro and Monte Bove Sud opens up SE. The descent continues in wide curves across dry terrain anchored by strips of conifers in an attempt at reforestation. Loose crumbly scree is underfoot – watch your step. The path leads down to expanses of meadow and a fountain, where you turn R through oak woods on a rough gravel lane for the last leg to **Casali** (1hr 30mins, 1080m).

Rifugio Casali ☎ 0737 99590 or mob 347 4684901 sleeps 16, open weekends + July–Aug + on request; the guardian will pick up guests at Ussita www.rifugiocasali.com

Rifugio del Fargno ☎ mob 330 280690 or 0733 492872 (guardian's home) sleeps 14, no shower, open Aug + weekends June–Oct + on request.

WALK 7

Monte Priora

Walking time	4hrs 45mins
Difficulty	Grade 2–3
Ascent/descent	650m/650m
Distance	10.3km/6.4 miles
Start/Finish	Forcella del Fargno
Access	Forcella del Fargno is accessible by fairly decent dirt roads from both Pintura di Bolognola (6kms) and Casali (13kms). Both climb in wide and occasionally bumpy curves. Be aware that both heavy rain and prolonged dry spells (which cause rockfalls) can make them tricky – enquire locally. Hotel Bucaneve at Bolognola have a minibus and will drive guests up. On foot, in view of the distances it's only feasible if an overnight stay at Rifugio del Fargno is included – in any case follow either road or the path from Casali (Walk 6, map p100).

Rearing 2332 metres above sea level, namely the nearby Adriatic, Monte Priora is the conclusion of a momentous isolated ridge that breaks off from the Sibillini chain in the northern section. Its elegant triangular shape dominates the hills above Amandola. Monte Priora and its grassy surrounds were the property of the Camaldoli monks of San Leonardo in Gole dell'Infernaccio, and the mountain took its name from the community's leader, the prior. Access is long-winded from any direction, but the handiest is from Forcella del Fargno. Thanks to its hinge location between Val di Panico and Val di Fargno, this saddle affords magnificent views: firstly of Monte Bove Nord and Monte Rotonda, then of neighbouring mountains Pizzo Tre Vescovi and Pizzo Berro. The name Fargno (pronounce the 'gn' like 'ny') is believed to derive from *farnia*, a type of oak.

Val di Panico, Monte Bove Nord and Casali

The best part of this magnificent and rewarding route follows extremely high crests that are razor thin in places. While these may not seem particularly difficult in ascent, remember that on the way down the sensation of exposure will inevitably increase several fold, compounded by fatigue. Moreover it cannot be overemphasised that stable good weather, preferably with little or no wind, is key to this walk. It is advisable to wait until late summer to minimise the chances of encountering snow or ice en route. Lastly, copious amounts of drinking water and sun/wind protection are essential. ▶

For an easier route in this area, see Walk 6.

WALK

From **Forcella del Fargno** (1811m) and the eponymous bunker-cum-*rifugio*, follow the broad shoulder briefly due E to where a clear if narrow path breaks off R (SE). This climbs easily over the head of Val di Panico with its myriad dolinas at the foot of Monte Bove Nord. The vast views also take in the villages of Casali and Ussita.

The terrain is dry and colonised by hardy clumps of grass which provide shelter for ground-nesting birds. At the southern base of Pizzo Tre Vescovi you reach the saddle of **Forcella Angagnola** (1924m, 30mins) where magnificent views towards the Piceno plain can be admired, along with the walk destination, bulky Monte Priora. A cluster of stones acts as signposting for path numbers.

Over the head of Valle dell'Ambro follow the broad ridge SSE towards the forbidding rock point of Pizzo Berro. While not carrying the usual red/white waymarks, the path is clear if arduous, climbing initially on the R side of the ridge to avoid rock outcrops. Further up it moves onto the ridge itself, continuing steadily to the **2150m** mark.

Variant via Pizzo Berro (30mins extra)
Experts only can stay on the ridge from the 2150m mark and continue uphill to the 2259m point of **Pizzo Berro**. Then, taking great care on the steep exposed terrain, there's a clambering descent via the NE crest. This joins the main route at the **2110m saddle** for the subsequent ascent of Monte Priora.

Here you fork L (SSE) onto easier terrain across the steep grassed Pianella Regina pasture slopes, detouring well below Pizzo Berro. In the company of crickets and yellow gentians, you curve NE and dip to a **2110m saddle** (1hr), joining the strategic ridge that links Pizzo Berro with Monte Priora. Here the southern flank is a breathtaking plunge to the Val Tenna with the Infernaccio gorge, while ahead are Monte Sibilla (SE) and Porche (S).

Now it's due E, straight up the razor sharp shoulder for the final 222m climb, watching your step. The prize is breathtaking **Monte Priora** with its iron cross (2332m, 45mins), the eastern extremity of the Sibillini, looking straight out to the Adriatic Sea. To the S the elegant dome of the Corno Grande in Abruzzo's Gran Sasso stands out.

Return the same way to **Forcella Angagnola** (1924m, 1hr 30mins) then **Forcella del Fargno** (1811m, 30mins).

Heading up Monte Priora

Rifugio del Fargno ☎ mob 330 280690 or 0733 492872 (guardian's home) sleeps 14, no shower, open daily in Aug + weekends June–Oct + other times on request.

Casali: Rifugio Casali ☎ 0737 99590 or mob 347 4684901 sleeps 16, open weekends + July–Aug + on request; the guardian will pick up guests at Ussita www.rifugiocasali.com

Bolognola: Hotel Bucaneve ☎ 0737 520131

WALK 8

The Monte Bove Circuit

Walking time	5hrs
Difficulty	Grade 2–3
Ascent/descent	1050m/1050m
Distance	11km/6.8 miles
Start/Finish	Hotel Felycita, Frontignano
Access	Frontignano is a short drive from either Castelsantangelo or Ussita. A bus runs this far July–Aug from Ussita; at other times the hotels will pick up guests.

The modest ski resort of Frontignano, dating back to the 1960s skiing boom, has a handful of hotels and is the perfect base for this superb high-altitude circuit of the Monte Bove peaks. Beginning in thick beech woods, the route climbs into glacially modelled Val di Bove, which is majestically crowned by the south and north points of Monte Bove along with the elongated slab of Monte Bicco. This magnificent valley is invisible from outside. Its broad outer rim is followed in a vast semi-circle of scenic ridges which afford magnificent views of the entire Sibillini range whichever way you look. The route meets with countless ups and downs and several drawn-out stretches that feel exposed, wholly unsuitable in high winds as the gusts can knock walkers off their feet, a dangerous possibility. A very worthwhile substitute in adverse windy weather is the shorter, easier Grade 2, 3hr loop that avoids the exposed crests. Though less panoramic, for obvious reasons, it is, nevertheless, rewarding – see below. ◂

A group of Apennine chamois was released on Monte Bove in 2009 and the north summit is currently strictly out of bound to walkers. The path skirts the area – do not leave it at any time. With binoculars you may be lucky to spot one of these elegant endangered creatures.

Midsummer walkers may like to take advantage of the Selvapiana chairlift in descent on the last leg from Rifugio Cristo delle Nevi, a saving of 30mins.

A note on a name: commonly assumed to mean oxen (*buoi* in Italian), Bove actually derives from *bovo* for stone.

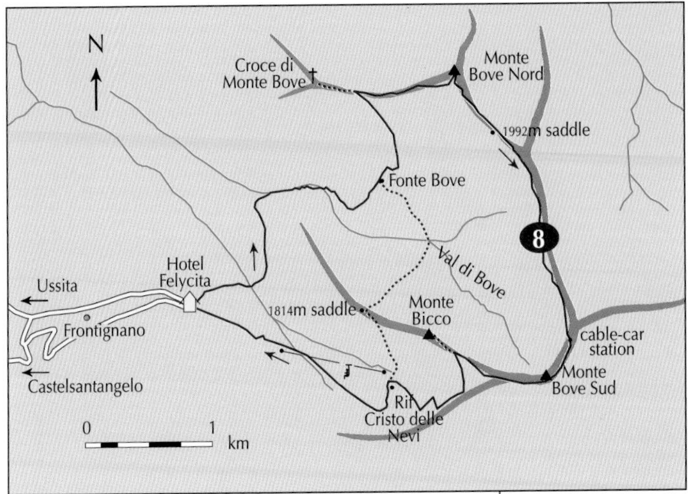

WALK

On the north side of **Hotel Felycita** (1325m) a lane breaks off ENE in gentle descent into the Macchie di Bicco, lovely beech woods with the odd conifer. Encounters with orange lilies as well as roe deer are likely. Path n.272 bears N to round outliers of Monte Bicco before a steeper uphill stretch due E as it enters the vast amphitheatre of Val di Bove. At fenced-in **Fonte Bove** (1hr 20mins, 1597m) the shorter loop forks off.

Shorter loop via Monte Bicco saddle (1hr)

From **Fonte Bove** (1597m) continue SE on clear path n.272 past sheep and horses at pasture. Without actually going all the way to the upper glacial basin, it soon swings SW and ascends gently to a clear notch in the rocky backbone of Monte Bicco at a **1814m saddle**. Here is a marvellous outlook beyond Frontignano to isolated Monte Cardosa. Ignore the ridge route L and continue SSE in easy descent across a minor valley and up to the chair lift at **Rifugio Cristo delle Nevi** snack bar, not far from a huge white statue and the main route.

Ascending Val di Bove

Turn L (NE) from the enclosure on the faint path, keeping away from the trees and making your way up to where a clear unnumbered path is encountered, cutting the grassy slopes N-NW. After a steady, problem-free ascent the crest is gained at a 1880m junction (40mins), almost directly above Casali and Torrente Ussita and opposite Monte Rotondo.

Optional side trip to Croce di Monte Bove (20mins return)
This recommended but not mandatory side trip leads W along an airy crest to the iron cross **Croce di Monte Bove** (1905m), in an amazing location looking over the glorious hills of Umbria.

Turn R (due E) via a modest saddle and up the grassy ridge, keeping to the R side. After an outcrop, the path as such disappears and you make your own way up the gentian-studded grass slope to breathtaking **Monte Bove Nord** (2112m, 30mins). Brilliant views range beyond

View across the central Sibillini near Monte Bove Sud (Walk 7)

The wonderful panorama here looks S over the central Sibillini with Monte Porche, and further to Monte Vettore, then close at hand across Val Tenna to Monte Sibilla.

Pizzo Tre Vescovi and Pizzo Berro all the way across the Piceno hills to the Adriatic coast.

When you've had your fill, head SSE down the slope to a **1992m saddle**, and up again, inspired by the Val di Panico below and elongated Pizzo Berro. The long gentle ascent concludes at an abandoned **cable-car station** (2148m, 1hr), legacy of the '60s skiing frenzy, erected at great expense and never used due to an error of positioning (someone evidently forgot to take the extreme wind factor into account). ◂

A clear path now moves off SSW, sticking to the easier L side of the ridge across flowered, rocky terrain, rather narrow and a little exposed at times. It takes in **Monte Bove Sud** (2169m), though the summit is hardly evident. Accompanied by plunging views to the head of Val di Bove, you touch on an old cable-car pylon and soon reach a saddle (2020m, 20mins) in the vicinity of the rocky ridge of Monte Bicco.

Side trip to Monte Bicco (30min return)

Continue WNW up the rocky crest for the short clamber to the rocky top of **Monte Bicco** (2052m), perched on the dizzy southern edge of Val di Bove. Return to the 2020m saddle afterwards.

Turn L (SE) on the clear path in descent to the top of a ski lift. Not far below is another lift with a bar (closed in summer). A wider white track now goes R (WNW) – *ignore* the red/white markings that soon branch off L – to the bottom of the defunct cable-car and **Rifugio Cristo delle Nevi** (1830m, 25mins, midsummer snack bar). The shorter loop via the Monte Bicco saddle slots in here. Close-by is a white statue of Christ with outstretched arms, a handy landmark. (The Selvapiana chair lift here usually operates in midsummer; it terminates on the lane a short stroll from Hotel Felycita.)

Just S of the statue leave the track to make your way down into the grassy fold of a minor valley below the northern flank of Monte Cornaccione. An unmarked path

Cristo delle Nevi

quickly becomes clear and a fun scree-running descent NW ensues. Orchids and bellflowers brighten the grassy surrounds. As you reach the wood, red/white markings appear for path n.271. Further down, these point you L to the chair lift arrival station then a lane. It's not far in gentle descent back to the start point at **Hotel Felycita** (1325m, 45mins).

Frontignano: Hotel Felycita ☎ 0737 90209 www.hotelfelycita.com
Domus Laetitiae ☎ 0737 90140 open mid-June to Sept www.domus laetitiae.it

WALK 9

Gole dell'Infernaccio

Walking time	3hrs 45mins
Difficulty	Grade 2
Ascent/descent	600m/600m
Distance	13.5km/8.3 miles
Start/Finish	car park 2km E of Rubbiano
Access	The tiny hamlet of Rubbiano is located on a signed turn-off from the Amandola–Montemonaco road.

Be aware that the Gole dell'Infernaccio is one of the most visited places in the Sibillini, so it's unreasonable to expect to have the paths to yourself.

One of the most exciting gorges in central Italy, the Gole dell'Infernaccio (Gorge of Hell!) slices through towering limestone cliffs on the eastern flanks of the range. The contrast with the bare treeless ridges of the innermost Sibillini couldn't be more striking. The dark, sunless recesses of the valley were daunting places for ancient travellers crossing the mountains via Passo Cattivo 'bad col', in the olden days. The appellation Infernaccio ('worse than hell'), speaks for itself. Modern-day walkers need not fear as the narrowest passages have been fitted with timber walkways and handrails. A final name: Tenna, the river which has been responsible for excavating the canyon, in all likelihood derived from the supreme Etruscan divinity Tinia (Jupiter for the Romans).

En route, a side path climbs to the lovely setting of San Leonardo and its church, once a helpful stopover on the strategic route linking the innermost Sibillini valleys to the Adriatic coast. A community of Camaldolesi monks set up shop here in the 9th century with a total of 24 brothers and a graceful Romanesque church, but were forced to abandon the site in the 1500s in the face of insurmountable hardships. Then in the 1960s a lone priest made the spot his hermitage and set about building a new church, stirring up a

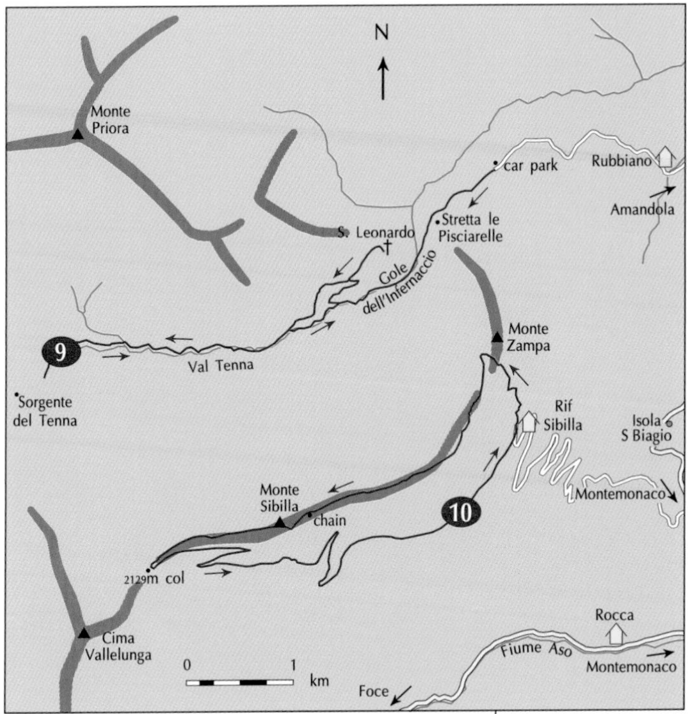

storm of controversy (well, he did demolish the historical one to replace it with a modern structure, and this is a National Park).

This walk coincides with the park route E10.

WALK

After the **car park** beyond Rubbiano (953m), the dirt road is closed to unauthorised traffic. Here the valley is hemmed in by towering limestone cliffs belonging to Monte Zampa (S) and Il Pizzo (N), a promise of even better things to come. Lined with scented elderberry trees and broom shrubs, the clear 4WD track n.221 moves SW into **Stretta le Pisciarelle**, where waterfalls

Approaching the Gole dell'Infernaccio

drip in curtains from a mossy ledge. Dominated by yawning cliffs, the Fiume Tenna is soon crossed on a footbridge (845m) and a path climbs to the L of a tunnel (used by forestry commission vehicles). It's only metres to the start of the exciting gorge. ▶ The smooth, sculpted rock faces are the result of centuries of water gushing down the valley and slowly carving out its own path.

Dwarfed by amazing cliffs and cooled by fresh breezes from the stream, the path weaves its way across a series of bridges and walkways over icy blue cascades.

As the cliffs broaden a little and woods take over, the 4WD track reappears. A signed fork points R (NW) for the short zigzagging climb through divine beech woodland to the church of **San Leonardo** (1hr, 1128m). It's a good viewpoint S towards Monte Sibilla as well as downstream.

A short way back down the ascent path, instead of returning immediately to the valley floor, turn R on the clear but unmarked path WSW. Overgrown in spots it gradually descends to the main valley track. This criss-crosses the delightful cascading stream, often in the shade of soaring cliffs pitted with natural cavities. The undergrowth features swathes of purple orchids and bright orange lilies. A fair way along, the path climbs steeply away from the stream and over two rises. Clumps of peonies thrive on the banks as open pasture commences, dotted with bushes of dog roses. A hut is passed, then a drinking trough. Only minutes further on, at the confluence of two valleys at the foot of Cima Cannafusto is **Sorgente del Tenna** (1hr 15mins, 1178m), aka Capotenna, source of the Fiume Tenna. A tap supplies deliciously cool spring water. The surroundings are a tad disappointing, however, as the main spring has been piped for the district water supply, hence the low concrete construction. Moreover the area is well used by cattle. The good news is the great views the spot affords of the ridges and peaks crowning the upper valley, including the north face of Monte Sibilla, as well as the upper Valle Lunga, which terminates due S with Monte Porche. The track actually continues W to Passo Cattivo.

Return to the **car park** (1hr 30mins, 953m) via the main valley track.

Entering the Gole dell'Infernaccio

Agriturismo Le Castellare ☎ 0736 856270 www.lecastellare.it
B&B Ca' de la Rossa (☎ 333 8412523 www.bbcadelarossasibillini.jimdo.com) is a convenient substitute for the still-unopened rifugio here.

WALK 10

Monte Sibilla Circuit

Walking time	4hrs
Difficulty	Grade 2–3
Ascent/descent	633m/633m
Distance	11km/6.8 miles
Start/Finish	Rifugio Sibilla
Access	Between Montemonaco and Isola San Biagio a good, if unsurfaced, gravel road forks W for the winding 6km climb to Rifugio Sibilla. The nearest public transport is at Montemonaco. Local taxi ☎ 0736 856380 or mob 333 3702593. Walk map on p115.

An extremely enjoyable loop walk via the most mythical mountain in the Sibillini, with amazing panoramas.

As long back as anyone can remember, flat-topped mountain Monte Sibilla, on the eastern flanks of the range, was reputed to be the dwelling place of a sibyl, a prophetess who was famed for her wisdom across Europe. Literature and art depict her as either a wicked witch or benevolent beautiful queen, with a retinue of gorgeous enchantresses who could transform themselves into horrible snakes when the need arose. A nicer story tells how they would dash down to the villages in their free time to dance the night away with luckless males, easy prey abandoned before first light, as the girls, alias fairies or *fate*, had to be back home before their cloven hoofs became evident. There was also talk of erotic rituals, and scholars have suggested a basis in history: the 'Brothers and Sisters of the Free Spirit' movement bloomed here 1344–1428; in all likelihood they were persecuted by envious neighbours.

The sibyl was also reputed to possess inestimable riches, kept in her cave home deep within the mountain. Still today old people in the neighbouring villages will tell visitors about the curious hole in the mountaintop they peered into as children and the cool air that came

Rifugio Sibilla

forth. Optimistic treasure expeditions as recently as 1953 by Belgians reported only a disappointing 16th-century coin, a spur and a knife. Unfortunately, over-enthusiastic attempts to locate the riches also involved dynamite, and these days the cave entrance is an impenetrable hole blocked with stones. Monte Sibilla suffered more unwarranted and irreversible damage in the 1960s when a road was gouged out of its impervious southern flank, purportedly to encourage development of pastureland. Left unfinished, it is visible from afar, a giant permanent zigzag scar, a Zorro sword flash.

In terms of the walk, the outward stretch follows crests, so views are far-reaching and non-stop, then the return leg takes a broad if rough track back to Rifugio Sibilla. Two brief sections require a sure foot and lack of vertigo. The first is the short rope-aided climb onto the summit crown of the mountain while the second, a tad longer, goes along a crumbly narrow crest and is a bit hairy. The latter can always be avoided by turning around and retracing your steps. There is no shade at all on this walk, so sun protection and drinking supplies are indispensable. On the other hand, at all costs avoid the route in a strong wind.

An overnight stay is feasible at Rifugio Sibilla, a dull brick building in a superb location. High on the eastern flank of Monte Sibilla, it gazes out E over rolling hills towards the Adriatic Sea taking in modest Monte Ascensione, said to be the launching pad for Christ's ascent into heaven. Due S is the cluster of peaks belonging to the Vettore group.

WALK

From the fountain at the rear of **Rifugio Sibilla** (1540m) a path climbs up the grassy slope. A second tap is passed and a shrine reached. Now, marked with red/white paint stripes, path n.155 proceeds N in easy curves, bearing W to gain a long crest at 1760m, adjacent to Monte Zampa. Here the ground drops away at your feet as there's a dizzy plunge to Val Tenna with the Infernaccio gorge. Towering NW is Monte Priora. N.155 turns L (SW) along the high crest colonised with prostrate juniper shrubs, running a tad under the actual ridge line and touching on a couple of saddles. Views are simply amazing: S over the village of Foce in the perfect U-shaped Valle del Lago di Pilato that terminates with Monte Vettore and its neighbours, while beyond rise Monti della Laga and Gran Sasso. The going is straightforward as the pink-tinged castle-like summit section of Monte Sibilla is approached. Here a distinct rock band crowns the elongated mountain, and walkers scramble up, aided by a **fixed rope** (2102m). Now across a broad grassy slope the path touches on a deep hole obstructed with fallen stones, erstwhile entrance to the amazing enchanted kingdom of the famous sibyl. Close at hand is the top of **Monte Sibilla** (1hr 50mins, 2173m), marked by a metal plaque, a rather dizzy if panoramic spot with an outlook both towards the Adriatic Sea and the inland Sibillini ridges. In summer the air up here is thick with swarms of insects and swallows.

Scrambling up to the crown on Monte Sibilla

▸ Now proceed carefully due W along the slim ridge, which is exposed on both sides. This gradually widens, descending to more stable terrain where pretty, white rock jasmine blooms among the grass. Curious natural trenches and pretty trumpet flowers accompany the path to a **2129m col** (30mins) and path junction, not to mention 4WD track. The ridge route continues SW via Cima Vallelunga and all the way to Monte Porche (see Walk 11), while another path, albeit faint, plunges N to Val Tenna. However for the purposes of this route you veer L (E) for the surprisingly steep track that makes its way down the southern flank of Monte Sibilla. Though a little monotonous, it is easy walking and leaves plenty of time to appreciate the Valle del Lago di Pilato again. After a shepherds' hut the track bears ENE and coasts back to **Rifugio Sibilla** (1hr 40mins, 1540m), which remains out of sight until the very last moment.

Note: the following 10mins follow an exposed ridge – if it doesn't look like your cup of tea then turn back here and retrace your steps to Rifugio Sibilla.

Rifugio Sibilla ☎ 0736 856422 or mob 338 4292399 sleeps 35, open May to Sept. www.rifugiosibilla1540.com.

WALK 11

Monte Porche and Palazzo Borghese

Walking time	4hrs
Difficulty	Grade 2 (Monte Porche Grade 2–3, avoidable)
Ascent/descent	700m/700m
Distance	11.6km/7.2 miles
Start/Finish	Hotel La Baita
Access	Either a winding drive south of Castelsantangelo sul Nera, or north from Castelluccio, is the road pass Forca di Gualdo, aka Madonna della Cona. From here a good road turns E for 2km, terminating at guesthouse La Baita and an ample car park.

Two great walkers' peaks with awesome vistas are twinned in this wonderfully rewarding route. No particular difficulties are involved, leaving walkers free to admire successive far-reaching views.

Gaining the lofty central ridges of the Sibillini generally requires concerted effort and ascents of near-mammoth proportions, from low-altitude valley departure points. This route is the exception, thanks to the good surfaced road that branches off from Forca di Gualdo to the winter ski zone of Monte Prata. Moreover the position of Monte Porche and Palazzo Borghese at the halfway point along the range ensures superb views over peaks and valleys in all directions. A further bonus is the stunning array of wildflowers encountered; rare Apennine edelweiss heads the list, which continues with gentians, pretty carnivorous butterwort, pink thrift and carline thistles.

Curious place names abound here: Porche is unrelated to the automobile company but to 'pig', possibly boar. The name Palazzo Borghese on the other hand, 'bourgeois palace', apparently dates back to Roman times, though its name has been somewhat fancifully linked with a long-gone palace erected on the peak.

At the walk start is a lovely, newly refurbished guesthouse. It is run by the family of a renowned endurance speleologist who has even excavated several underground rooms here. Otherwise, beautifully located on

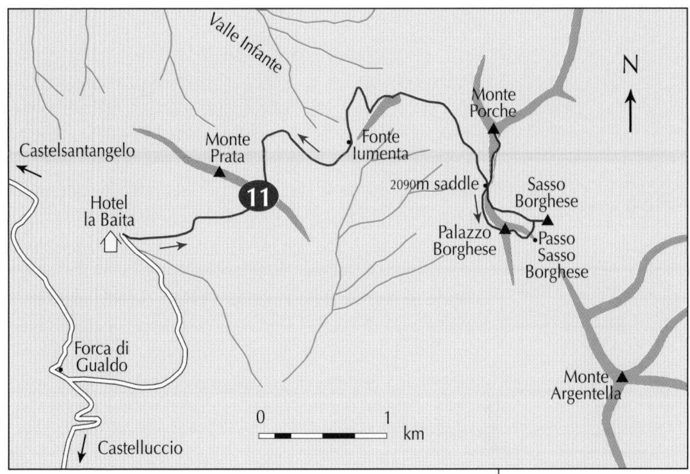

the panoramic road above Castelsantangelo sul Nera, is Hotel La Fiorita at Spina di Gualdo.

Mist-filled Piano Grande from Fonte Iumenta

WALK

From the car park at **Hotel La Baita** (1651m), take the unsurfaced lane E at first, past drinking troughs below modest Monte Prata dotted with ski lifts. Breathtaking views sweep over the Piano Grande with Castelluccio on its perch, and edged by the Cima del Redentore standing out SE. After several changes of direction, it concludes at the drinking troughs of **Fonte Iumenta** (mare's spring) (1799m). A clear well-graded path marked with red paint splashes now heads L (NE) climbing high over Valle Infante, with marvellous views of both Castelsantangelo sul Nera and Monte Cardosa. Though dry and stony here, there are profusions of milk vetch, carline thistles and clumps of mouse-ear, not to mention noisy crickets. A wide curve points SSE for a coast to a scenic **2090m saddle** (1hr 30mins).

Looming overhead NNE is Monte Porche, the next destination. Should it not look like your cup of tea, skip this section (saving 30mins) and proceed for Palazzo Borghese. Leave the path and turn L (N) up the steepish flanks with thrift flowers. Near the top the odd pole marks the way around a rock outcrop and up to **Monte Porche** (2233m), which feels like the summit of the world of the Sibillini. In fact it gives an excellent idea of the make-up of the system of narrow ridges and deep plunging valleys that constitute this central Apennine mountain range, as well as the closeness of the Adriatic Sea. Retrace your steps to the **2090m saddle** (30mins).

Cut across the arrival route and leave the path, heading R (S) along the L side of the ensuing ridge. This takes you to the modest elevation of **Palazzo Borghese** (2145m) with extraordinary bird's-eye views over the expanse of the Piano Grande and the eastern realms of the Sibillini with the Vettore-Redentore duo. Accompanied by choughs, who glide around optimistically hoping for visitor crumbs, continue E amidst veritable carpets of Apennine edelweiss. Descent from this rocky crest is via its eastern flank, dropping quickly to **Passo Sasso Borghese** (2057m, 30mins). Here are heart-stopping views down a funnel-shaped gully to Pian delle

En route to Monte Porche

Cavalle, dominated by the oblique strata that make up isolated **Sasso Borghese**. By all means follow the faint narrow path that ascends this curious 2119m outcrop, taking care on the exposed topmost stretch (15mins return time).

The return path NW threads its way through a sequence of dolinas, bowl-shaped depressions where the surface water drains underground, cutting the northern flank of Palazzo Borghese. It touches on the **2090m saddle** (30mins), whence downhill for Fonte Iumenta and back to the car park at **La Baita** (1651m, 1hr 15mins).

Hotel La Baita ☎ mob 333 6945392 www.monteprata.it
Spina di Gualdo: Hotel La Fiorita ☎ 0737 98331

WALK 12

Nocelleto to Forca di Gualdo

Walking time	4hrs
Difficulty	Grade 2–3
Ascent/descent	1120m/347m
Distance	10.3km/6.4 miles
Start/Finish	Nocelleto/Forca di Gualdo
Access	The quiet hamlet of Nocelleto is a mere 1.5km south of Castelsantangelo sul Nera. This village is accessible by year-round bus from Visso. Drivers have the choice of approach via the shady road along Valnerina river valley from Visso or the dramatic switchbacks of the road from Castelluccio via Forca di Gualdo.

The walk is unsuitable in inclement weather as poor visibility would make it difficult to get your bearings, landmarks being few and far between.

In a little-frequented valley of the Sibillini Park this superb if long extended traverse ascends through woods and over open crests that offer inspirational wide-reaching views. Shy roe deer, wild boar and birds of prey frequent the area, and masses of wildflowers brighten the grassy slopes. Old mule tracks are followed initially, but the paths on the higher reaches often disappear and extra time should be allowed for hunting around for the route.

This is the central part of the Sibillini. In contrast to the vast open altopiano and rocky ridges of the spiny chain, here are deep impervious valleys with wild flanks, thickly wooded. Human settlements are few and far between, small yet solid. Beyond Nocelleto, where the walk starts, stretches the Valle di Rapegna; the name derives from ancient Etruscan, a sign that those sophisticated pre-Roman people had settled in the district.

At the walk start in the valley hamlet of Nocelleto (a reference to walnut trees), is excellent-value family-run Albergo Il Navigante. Italian visitors flock here to dine on the luscious home-bred lamb. Otherwise, there is Hotel

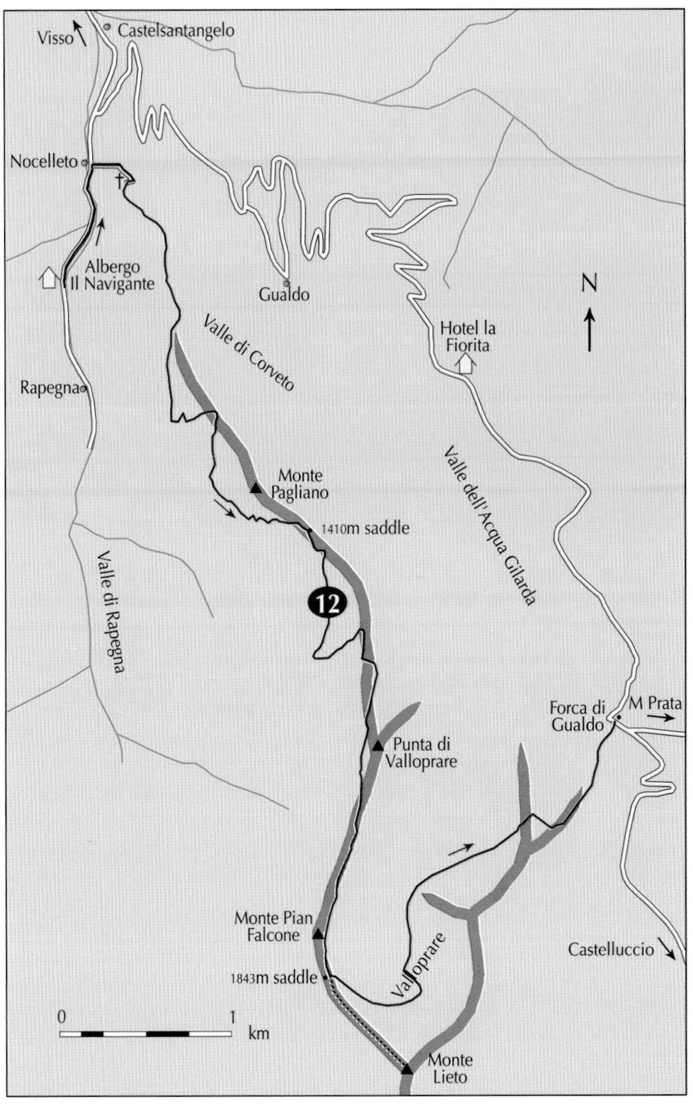

Visso
Castelsantangelo
Nocelleto
Albergo Il Navigante
Gualdo
N
Hotel la Fiorita
Valle di Corveto
Rapegna
Valle dell' Acqua Gilarda
Monte Pagliano
1410m saddle
Valle di Rapegna
12
Forca di Gualdo
M Prata
Punta di Valloprare
Monte Pian Falcone
Valloprare
Castelluccio
1843m saddle
0
1
km
Monte Lieto

Setting out from Nocelleto

La Fiorita, set on the scenic Spina di Gualdo ridge overlooking both Valle Infante and the walk route.

Note: the original plan was for a complete circuit walk, dropping on path n.253 via Valle dell'Acqua Gilarda and back to Nocelleto. Unfortunately this is not currently possible due to damage caused by avalanches and rockfalls, which has made the path impassable. It's worth enquiring at the Castelsantangelo sul Nera Park Visitor Centre to check if the situation has changed. Otherwise, to return to Nocelleto (and if you can't leave a car at the Forca di Gualdo road pass) arrange for a member of the hotel staff to pick you up, or else plan on hitchhiking back.

WALK

Downhill from Albergo Il Navigante at **Nocelleto** (741m), turn E on the narrow road signposted for *Casa di riposo* (old people's home). It quickly climbs in curves to the converted monastery and 13th-century church Santa Maria Castellare. Just before the buildings, red/white

Last leg to Monte Pian Falcone

markings n.252 and 'N' for the *sentiero natura* (park nature trail) point L (SE) up a steep old lane. The marked way rises steadily along a lightly wooded ridge that divides the Valle di Rapegna from Valle dell'Acqua Gilarda, with several villages visible. At first the vegetation is Mediterranean in nature with broom and aromatic herbs, alternating with patches of chestnut and beech trees with cyclamens. About half an hour on, ignore the lane that breaks off L for Valle di Corveto, and keep R (still n.252) due S with outlooks over the hamlet of Rapegna and bare-topped Monte Cardosa. The gradient steepens considerably and a series of old lanes and paths is followed. At 1060m, as shown on the maps, keep your eyes peeled for a cairn denoting a fork L for a less obvious mule track. This emerges at a lookout (1200m) over Castelsantangelo sul Nera, the inverted 'V' shape of its castle walls standing out clearly on the mountainside. The lane peters out here and you need to veer R (S) for a faintly marked path that avoids the top of Monte Pagliano. Then ensure you climb due E over a grassy slope punctuated with prickly juniper shrubs and bright blue-purple eryngo to a broad **1410m saddle** (1hr 45mins). Across Valle dell'Acqua Gilarda, Hotel La Fiorita can be seen on the roadside while NNE is the Bove line-up, and Monte Porche E with Palazzo Borghese beyond rounded Monte Prata.

A fairly obvious path heads S up the mountainside into a beech copse. As it is about to leave the shade of the trees the path veers abruptly L (NE) and up to open mountainsides at 1584m with vast views. A useful landmark here is an old eroded milestone (don't waste time looking for Casale Brandi, marked on the 1:25,000 map, as it is a mere heap of stones off the route). Both path and waymarks disappear for a while but you keep L (S) above the tree line and up the vast backbone, heading inexorably for the top of Punta di Valloprare, though its 1776m top is detoured to the west. A decent path reappears for the steady climb up the incredibly panoramic ridge of **Monte Pian Falcone**, twittering skylarks everywhere. A conspicuous cairn marks the **1843m saddle** (1hr 15mins) where stunning all-round vistas can be admired, starting SW with Monte Patino, recognisable by its summit cross. On top of the world – with the sheep and birds of prey.

Extension to Monte Lieto (20mins)
For improved views over Piano Grande and Castelluccio, proceed SE along the crest to 1944m **Monte Lieto**. Afterwards either return to the **1843m saddle** or cut N down the grassy slopes, taking special care not to miss the faint path for the descent route.

Ignore the marked path that proceeds S but instead swing L – initially E – curving below Monte Lieto into Valloprare and above a small dam used by livestock. A clear path (n.251) curves down NE, leaving this inner valley. Further on, in sight of the road pass, it cuts across very steep grassy slopes and drops to a beautiful beech wood with gnarled old trees, many bent to unnatural angles by winter avalanches. A patch of

Beech trees bent by avalanches

conifers precedes the arrival at the road pass **Forca di Gualdo** (1496m, 1hr) and its copious drinking fountain. Overlooking Pian Perduto 'lost plain', the tiny shrine of Madonna della Cona commemorates a terrible battle in 1522 between the folk of Visso and those of Norcia, remembered on the first Sunday in July – Walk 18 gives more gory detail.

Nocelleto: Albergo Il Navigante ☎ 0737 98106 www.dalnavigante.it
Spina di Gualdo: Hotel La Fiorita ☎ 0737 98331

WALK 13

Preci and Sant'Eutizio

Walking time	3hrs
Difficulty	Grade 1–2
Ascent/descent	520m/520m
Distance	9.7km/6 miles
Start/Finish	Preci
Access	Buses from Norcia serve Borgo and Preci on a regular basis. By car you need the minor road between Valnerina and Norcia.

An excellent half-day loop walk in the lovely wooded and pastoral surroundings of minor Val Castoriana.

It starts out in Valle del Campiano at the charming Umbrian village of Preci, believed to have taken its name from 'precipice' due to its position on a steep hillside, though it may be related to an old monastery. The walk passes through Borgo before traversing easy hillsides bright with wildflowers. Then, built into the hillside in a secluded valley is the fine Romanesque abbey of Sant'Eutizio, an inspiring spot to visit. Afterwards a return is made through woodland thick with the scent of Mediterranean plants.

Walking is straightforward, but take care on the downhill return stretch to Borgo as the path disappears for a little while. On the whole there is very little waymarking to speak of, despite the optimistic profusion of numbered paths on commercial maps. In terms of practicalities, Borgo has grocery shops and an ATM, while Preci has a lovely hotel. Both are served by bus. The restaurant at Sant'Eutizio also has rooms for guests.

This district was the stage for some fascinating episodes in medical history. In the 16th–17th centuries Preci was home to illustrious surgeons who learnt the delicate arts of removing cataracts and kidney stones and performing hernia operations from the expert monks of Sant'Eutizio, after the latter were forbidden from

Courtyard at Sant'Eutizio abbey

practising, in the 1400s, by ecclesiastical edict. Their talents were in great demand at the courts of Europe and the East to treat emperors, sultans, kings and even Queen Elisabeth I. According to local hearsay, the diligent Precians perfected techniques through practice on pigs, which incidentally made them expert butchers, contributing to the district's reputation for making delicious sausages in the Norcia tradition. Ancient instruments are on display in a museum at Sant'Eutizio.

The monastery itself was founded in AD470 by San Spes (Sant'Eutizio was his follower) on a site occupied by cave-dwelling hermits as far back as the 3rd century. The order soon became specialised in herbal medicine and cutting-edge surgery. Sant'Eutizio was also credited with miracle-working: during long dry periods when water shortages became dire, his belt would be carried in procession, and on its arrival at the monastery the heavens inevitably burst open.

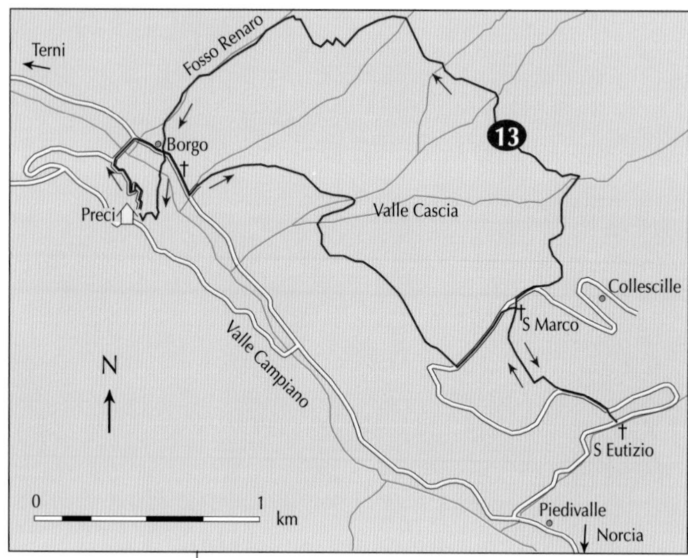

WALK

From the car park in upper **Preci** (596m) turn up alongside Hotel agli Scacchi, a 15th-century palace named after a prominent surgeon. In the peaceful pedestrian-only area, amidst historic buildings, you walk downhill on paved Via Cavalotti to a lower parking area. Turn L then almost immediately R for a lane to **Borgo** (532m) and the main road. Turn R (SE) for 5mins to the end of the village and past an overgrown shrine then L. This surfaced road soon reverts to a leafy lane E (this corresponds to n.186 on the SER map). At a fork and concrete wall (627m) keep R across Valle Cascia for the gentle climb out of beech woods onto open hillsides covered with masses of broom and exquisite wild orchids. Inspiring views range over the gently undulating hills and neighbouring farming valleys. At derelict farm buildings on a quiet road, turn L, with the hamlet of Collescille visible on a broom-splattered hillside. Soon after a picnic area go R on a path for the nearby shrine of **San Marco** (850m,

At Preci

1hr). Now, a shady, pleasant old path descends among oaks to reach a narrow road, then a belltower and cemetery where steep steps cut down the rock face to the beautiful Romanesque monastery of **Sant'Eutizio** (678m, 15mins).

The church and jasmine-draped courtyard are always accessible. However, should you strike lucky and be there when the inner precincts are open to the public, you'll also be able to inspect the ancient alchemist's laboratory where natural cures were concocted, as well as the collection of historical surgical instruments.

Walk back up to **San Marco** (850m, 20mins) and go R towards Collescille. Not far along, below the actual hamlet, turn L on a stony way frequently used by sheep, as your nose will tell you. At a patch of concrete paving with green metal poles, branch L (N) on a faint path through woods but on the upper edge of a field. The path quickly widens and faint red paint marks appear on rocks (shown as n.587 on the SER map). A lovely old route

At Sant'Eutizio

with the odd stretch of stone walling, it leads through holm oak woods alternating with rocky, sunny terrain with masses of aromatic herbs and broom. After a stream it bears NW on a level, cutting the SW flanks of Monte Moricone. There are occasional glimpses of Preci and wider views over Umbria.

A short way after a lengthy collapsed stretch of walling (approx. 875m), red stripes point you downhill on a steep rough track that ends in a field. (You have now well and truly left the n.587 shown on the SER map). Follow the top edge of the field around R and then down to where a clear track resumes R (NW) in steady descent. This feeds into a wider shady lane that sometimes doubles as a stream bed (lower **Fosso Renaro**) and reaches **Borgo** (532m, 1hr 10mins). On the opposite side of the road a path crosses a stream in the proximity of old channels constructed for the adjacent mill. An easy climb through woods emerges at a road, and it's not far back to the car park in upper **Preci** (596m, 15mins).

Preci: Hotel agli Scacchi ☎ 0743 99221 www.hotelagliscacchi.com. Good value establishment with the bonus of a swimming pool and delicious meals featuring regional cuisine.
Sant'Eutizio: Ristorante Biancofiore ☎ 0743 939319 or mobile ☎ 331 8163008 has reasonably priced guest rooms.

WALK 14

Monte Patino

Walking time	5hrs
Difficulty	Grade 2
Ascent/descent	875m/875m
Distance	12.8km/7.9 miles
Start/Finish	Forca d'Ancarano
Access	Buses on the Norcia–Preci run will let you off at Forca d'Ancarano, the high pass between the Norcia plain and Valle del Campiano. Cars can be parked in a lane just off the pass, taking care not to obstruct farm vehicles.

This wonderfully varied walk to a superbly panoramic mountaintop makes a great day out. Monte Patino stands isolated from the central Sibillini chain, making it a wonderful lookout towards its higher comrades as well as belvedere extraordinaire for the famous Umbrian walled town of Norcia and the rolling hills beyond. A circuit, it follows clear paths with easily identifiable marking and numbers. Early summer will guarantee brilliant spreads of wildflowers – a treat to be savoured. The walk start, Forca d'Ancarano, was once the site of an ancient Etruscan colony, though alas, nothing remains today.

Instead of completing the loop, it is possible to extend the route from the halfway point Forca di Giuda and proceed to Castelluccio, transforming this into a handy traverse walk (5hrs total – see below). A further recommended variant from the same pass is to slot into the GAS route and make the lovely long descent northwards to pretty Capo del Colle in Valle del Campiano, where a bus can be picked up (see GAS, Stage 7); this would make a total of 5hrs 35mins including Monte Patino.

View of Norcia from Monte Patino

WALK

At the road pass **Forca d'Ancarano** (1008m), the day's objective Monte Patino rises abruptly to the E. Take the clear lane (marked as park route E14) that turns up NW between wheat fields bright with poppies and cornflowers. At the first junction branch R, soon passing an old water trough. Not far on is a fork; n.581/E14 continues for Forca di Giuda but we go sharp L up a steep rocky track (n.582) that soon levels out as it heads N through light woodland. A gentle ascent ensues in the company of sweet broom shrubs and orchids; further on the way veers R (E) into peaceful Valle Ceresa. Stands of laburnum and beech give way to clearings carpeted with wild blooms, while above R (SE) looms Monte Patino, opposite Punta Venturetta L (N). In this green fold of a valley the beech trees are especially sheltered and they are consequently found as high as the 1600m level. Above that the path climbs across open grassy slopes to join the GAS route below the rounded hummock of Monte delle Rose. A short

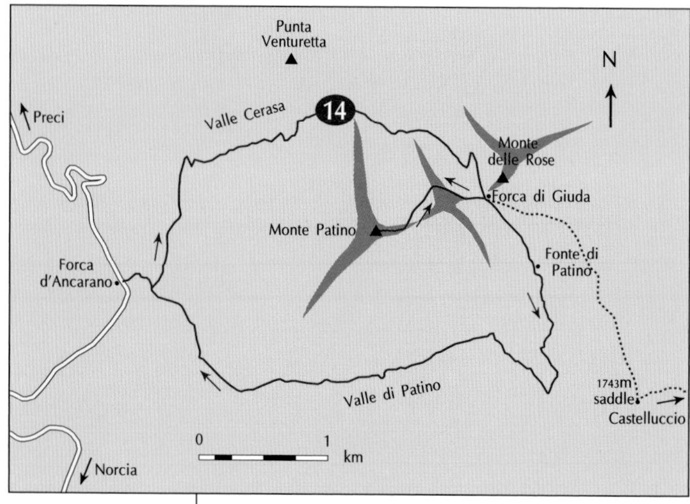

level stretch R brings you to the saddle **Forca di Giuda** (1794m, 2hrs 15mins).

Extension to Castelluccio (2hrs)
Follow the GAS route ESE over the broad crest under Monte delle Rose to where Walk 18 can be picked up at the **1743m saddle** for the wonderful traverse via Poggio di Croce (or the more straightforward gravel road at its base).

Now, n.582 heads due W, a lovely scenic coast via a minor col and up to the huge cross on **Monte Patino** (1883m, 25mins). The reward is the bird's-eye view SW over the walled town of Norcia, on its cultivated plain amidst the rolling hills of Umbria. In the opposite direction the inspiring peaks and crests of the central Sibillini ridge stretch out. Quite a spot!

Return the same way to **Forca di Giuda** (1794m, 20mins) and turn R in preparation for a plunge down n.581, the faint path R (SE) along a crumbly fault of

Approaching the summit of Monte Patino

multi-coloured rocks. Watch your step on the loose terrain. The gradient eases at **Fonte di Patino** (1557m), a spring with drinking troughs for livestock. A gentler descent follows S through beech copses before swinging NW to join a broad gravel track in upper Valle di Patino, fragrant with laburnum and broom. Between rock outcrops it levels out somewhat, finally curving past an abandoned quarry to the n.581/582 fork encountered on the outwards section. Here it's L for **Forca d'Ancarano** (1008m, 2hrs) once again.

The closest accommodation is at Norcia: Hostel Il Capisterium ☎ 0743 828616 www.norciaospitalita.it; for hotels contact ☎ 0743 816513 www.bianconi.com.

Otherwise at Preci there's Hotel agli Scacchi ☎ 0743 99221 www.hotelagliscacchi.com.

WALK 15

Foce and Lago di Pilato

Walking time	5hrs 30mins
Difficulty	Grade 2
Ascent/descent	1000m/1000m
Distance	14.6km/9 miles
Start/Finish	Foce
Access	From Montemonaco a quiet road ventures W up the Aso valley to the tiny village of Foce. The closest bus is at Montemonaco, with occasional services to Rocca. Local taxi ☎ 0736 856380 or mob 333 3702593.
Note	it is possible to drive past Foce along Piano della Gardosa for 2.5km to the 1100m mark and the end of the good unsurfaced road; this cuts 1hr 20mins off the walk total.

This memorable and extremely rewarding walk explores the fascinating Valle del Lago di Pilato, of great natural beauty.

A glacially formed U trough, it stretches N–S for 5km in a succession of stepped terraces that culminate in the crown of Sibillini peaks including Monte Vettore, the loftiest in the range. In the upper horseshoe cirque shelters much photographed Lago di Pilato, which has gradually shrunk to two bodies of water that resemble a pair of sunglasses. While extremely attractive – well, it is one of the rare lakes in the Sibillini – it is strictly off bounds for anything as tame as a paddle, let alone a dip. This cannot be over emphasised. The reason? Lago di Pilato is the one and only place in the world where the fairy shrimp *Chirocephalus marchesonii* lives, laying its eggs on the unreliable lake edge. The coral coloured creature grows 12–15mm in length and may be seen with the naked eye swimming tummy-up. But times have changed – in the past the lake had rather different inhabitants. In fact, so terrible was its reputation in the Middle Ages as home to devils and ghastly spirits,

The village of Foce and Monte Sibilla

attracting necromancers intent on unspeakable practices of devilry, that the church authorities thought fit to fence it in! But not before the inhabitants of Norcia undertook to sacrifice one of its inhabitants each year to appease the demons of the lake. And the name? As the story goes, Pontius Pilate was punished for his part in the death of Christ. He died in Rome, and oxen hauled his funeral cart from there to a high ridge, heaving his body into the depths of this lake which then took his cursed name. An even more fanciful version says the water turned red the moment Pilate washed his hands!

In practical terms, the walk itself entails a considerable climb of 1000 metres, but the path is always clear as it is well trodden. On hot summer days an early start is essential as there is no shade at all in the upper section. Carry food and plenty of drinking water, as the springs shown on maps cannot be relied upon. The valley floor is actually dry for the most part, as the little water there is flows mostly underground.

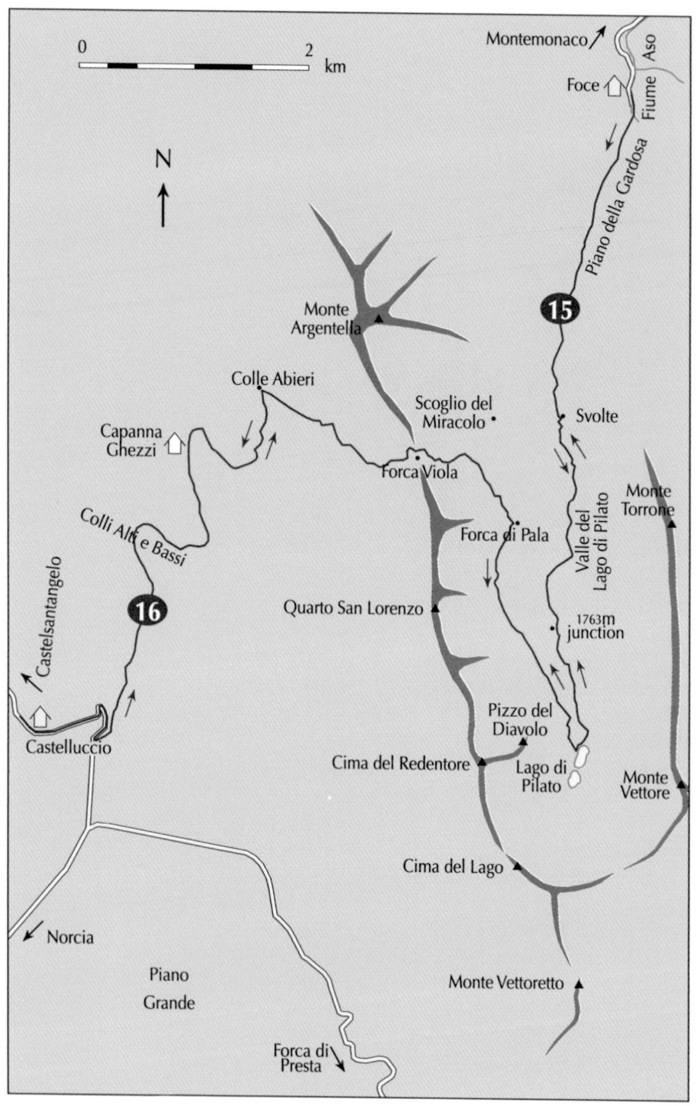
0
2
km
N
Montemonaco
Foce
Fiume Aso
Piano della Gardosa
15
Monte Argentella
Colle Abieri
Scoglio del Miracolo
Svolte
Capanna Ghezzi
Forca Viola
Monte Torrone
Valle del Lago di Pilato
Forca di Pala
Colli Alti e Bassi
Castelsantangelo
16
Quarto San Lorenzo
1763m junction
Pizzo del Diavolo
Castelluccio
Cima del Redentore
Lago di Pilato
Monte Vettore
Cima del Lago
Norcia
Piano Grande
Monte Vettoretto
Forca di Presta

Set beneath the southern side of Monte Sibilla, the start point Foce is a quiet rural hamlet encircled by scented lime trees. The name Foce is derived from the Latin for 'exit' – it is the source of the Fiume Aso, which is dammed downstream at Lago Gerosa. Foce has a decent family-run restaurant-cum-hotel with an outdoor café, though there's another establishment at Rocca, 3.5km away. Be aware that the valley is popular in July–August and can get busy, though of course at that time the amazing wildflowers are usually at their best.

WALK

Leave **Foce** (945m) on the road (also path n.151) out of the village due S across a bridge and past a gushing outlet for the Fiume Aso spring. The U-shape of this ancient glacial valley is immediately apparent, with its smooth cliffs on both sides. A 2km stretch in imperceptible ascent on the now unsurfaced lane traverses the flat pastures of Piano della Gardosa, the perfect habitat for pretty pyramidal orchids. Far ahead Pizzo del Diavolo rears its white rock point, while the valley appears obstructed by the imposing rock barrier Scoglio del Miracolo; here, according to legend, footholds appeared miraculously in aid of a bishop on horseback who lost his way. After traversing light woodland, all of a sudden the path becomes a steep climb through a wonderfully atmospheric gully bounded by soaring limestone cliffs. This stretch is known as the **Svolte** (1350m) or 'hairpin bends'. Loose stones underfoot combined with slippery leaves make the going tiring, but it's not far up to easier curves in shady beech woods, where lovely laburnum blooms. Once away from the glacially formed step and out of the tree cover, the path sticks to the centre of the narrow valley, where waist-high secondary vegetation indicates long-abandoned pasture. Continuing steadily uphill beneath Monte Torrone, you may notice the presence of green alder bushes, an indication of water – tiny Fonte Matta (1540m) in this case. Swinging briefly W around the knoll of Monte Rotondo the path traverses a sea of concentrated green which

Lago di Pilato

once hosted herders' huts (Capanna Piscini), mere heaps of stones nowadays. Not far on is the strategic **1763m junction** where n.153 forks R for Forca Viola (see Walk 16). Keep straight ahead on n.151, steadily uphill across loose stones. The final ascent prior to the lake is characterised by slopes dotted with dolinas which retain accumulated snow until remarkably late in the season. At last, dominated by soaring Pizzo del Diavolo W and Monte Vettore E, is fascinating **Lago di Pilato** (3hrs 15mins, 1940m). ◀

Cima del Lago closes the southern head of this lovely cirque where gay masses of yellow alpine woad thrives amidst the stones.

Afterwards, in descent, taking care on the rough steep stretches where ankles and knees are direly tested, allow 2hrs 15mins to retrace your steps back to **Foce** (945m).

Foce: Taverna della Montagna ☎ 0736 856327.
Rocca: Albergo Guerrin Meschino ☎ 0736 856218 www.guerrin meschino.com.

WALK 16

Castelluccio to Lago di Pilato

Walking time	6hrs 30mins
Difficulty	Grade 2
Ascent/descent	1020m/1020m
Distance	20.5km/12.7 miles
Start/Finish	Castelluccio
Access	Castelluccio can be reached by road from any of three directions – from Norcia, Visso and Castelsantangelo sul Nera or via Forca di Presta. The only bus comes from Norcia on Thursdays. Note: the lane as far as Capanna Ghezzi is rough and deeply rutted and only suitable for 4WDs. Walk map on p146.

A stunning if lengthy itinerary leading out of iconic Castelluccio on the beautiful Piano Grande to wild and wonderful Valle del Lago di Pilato.

The yawning U-shaped valley is entered from a panoramic lateral col, and many of the major Sibillini peaks are admired. Flower lovers who do the walk in summer will appreciate the brilliant spread of wildflowers that somehow flourish across the bare scree slopes. The walk destination is renowned Lago di Pilato, a photogenic if diminutive body of water, source of amazing legends and speculation over the centuries – see Walk 15.

Good, well-marked paths are followed all the way, and apart from summer weekends the valley does not see many visitors. Bear in mind though that the terrain is alpine in character and this is not a good place to get caught out in bad weather, as once Capanna Ghezzi is left behind there is no shelter at all. Also, carry food and plenty of drinking water as the springs cannot be relied on.

A fantastic way to do this route is in combination with Walk 15 which means a rewarding traverse from Castelluccio via the lake and down to Foce, in a total of 5hrs 45mins.

Mountain kidney-vetch growing on limestone

Capanna Ghezzi, passed en route and named after a wealthy landowner, is a comfortable bivouac hut, shared with shepherds but belonging to CAI Perugia; it can be booked – see below.

WALK

At **Castelluccio** (1452m) you need the clear lane at the southeastern foot of the village knoll, where the ground levels out at the foot of the lowest curve. Heading off N between fields, it threads its tortuous way through the imaginatively named Colli Alti e Bassi (hills high and low), and climbs ever so gradually to the pasture around **Capanna Ghezzi** (1hr, 1570m) and a gushing fountain. Faded red/white paint markings can be found on the corner of the building near a park noticeboard – there's no path as such, so head up the grassy slope NE and you'll soon spot the path climbing SE across treeless slopes. It then swings N to **Colle Abieri** where you fork R. With great views to Castelluccio, a grey scree traverse ensues to strategic saddle **Forca Viola** (1hr 10mins, 1936m), a fortuitous passage between Monte Argentella and Quarto San Lorenzo. A dizzy valley plunges at your feet, quite a contrast from the gentle, sloping landscape of the Piano Grande, now left far behind.

A good path descends, snaking its way E to coast above Scoglio del Miracolo, a rock barrier which earned its name when miraculous hoof-holds appeared in the

Lago di Pilato at the foot of Pizzo del Diavolo

cliff for a bishop on horseback who had taken a wrong turning! Incredibly, the village of Foce comes into view N at the foot of Monte Sibilla. With occasional ups and downs, this spectacular traverse cuts high over the Valle del Lago di Pilato, moving S. After **Forca di Pala** are extended blinding scree slopes worthy of the Italian Dolomites. Brilliant splashes of colour are provided by yellow poppies in the company of pretty alpine woad and alpine cabbage. Note that path n.153 actually forks L to join the main route from Foce at a **1763m junction**, however it means losing height so you're better off keeping SSE on the clear path. All the variants do eventually end up at the lake but it's a good rule to stick to the highest when forks are encountered.

The massive sheer face of Pizzo del Diavolo is approached, its 'devil's point' looming over the 'diabolical' **Lago di Pilato** (1hr 20mins, 1940m) which only comes into view at the very last moment. An unworldly spot, the twin lakes are dark green-blue gems, almost metallic, in dramatic contrast to the stark white scree surrounds. The top of this glacially formed cirque is closed in by aptly named Cima del Lago SW and Monte Vettore E, the highest peak in the Sibillini. Notices on fence posts politely request that visitors avoid treading on the shore, so as not to disturb the eggs of the extremely rare fairy shrimp *Chirocephalus marchesonii,* discovered here in 1954.

Unless you opt for the descent to Foce (see Walk 15), return the same way via Forca Viola to **Castelluccio** (3hrs, 1452m).

Castelluccio: Taverna di Castelluccio ☎ 0743 821158 www.taverna castelluccio.it
Locanda de' Senari ☎ 0743 821205 www.agriturismosenari.it
Capanna Ghezzi sleeps 12, CAI Perugia, available to self-sufficient walkers who are members of the Italian Alpine Club www.caiperugia.it.

WALK 17

Monte Vettore

Walking time	4hrs 15mins + 40mins extension
Difficulty	Grade 2
Ascent/descent	950m/950m
Distance	7.2km/4.5 miles
Start/Finish	Forca di Presta
Access	Road pass Forca di Presta is a short drive from Castelluccio, or a slightly longer one from either Norcia or Arquata del Tronto.

From Rifugio degli Alpini, near the road pass Forca di Presta, paths can clearly be seen in the north, snaking their way up the stone-ridden grass slopes that sweep down from high ridges. If you squint a bit, the tiny hut Rifugio Zilioli can be made out on the elongated col Sella delle Ciaule. Right of that is Monte Vettore, apparently square-shaped from this angle. The highest

Rifugio Zilioli

peak in the whole of the Monti Sibillini range, its name comes from the Latin for 'victor'. The highly recommended hike up there is surprisingly long and tiring, verging on 1000m in height gain. However, as these things go, all effort is amply repaid with breathtaking views stretching over the Sibillini and all the way to the glittering Adriatic coast.

An amusing series of stories circulate about controversial crosses erected on this mountain. In fact it was once known as Punta della Croce, after a huge iron exemplar placed on top in 1902. That lasted but one month, blown over by the usual strong Tramontana wind that howls through. However, the faithful were not to be so easily defeated and the following year drummed up more spiritual and financial support for an even more showy construction – a cross 20m tall, atop a masonry base-cum-shelter. But the gusts won again, toppling the monument, which smashed to smithereens far below, only to be recycled – fashioned into useful farming implements, hoes and horseshoes – by the inventive locals. These days a very modest cross marks the peak.

Should the summit walk not be enough for one day, by all means allow extra time and energy (only 65 extra metres down and up) for the tempting extension to a belvedere ridge over wondrous Lago di Pilato. (This body of water is barely glimpsed from the top of Monte Vettore). Whatever shrunken state that may be in – most likely twin crescents of deep blue water reminiscent of a pair of sunglasses – it's a delight, especially in this rugged mountain landscape where karsism is rife, and bodies of water, however small, provide rare pleasure. Other walks that visit the lake from close quarters are 15 and 16.

Warning: it goes without saying that it is inadvisable to embark on this route in a strong wind as the summit can be extremely dangerous.

Before starting out, pop down to the spring under the W side of the road pass to fill drinking bottles. ◂ A final note: en route, beautifully positioned at 2240m is Rifugio Zilioli, a spartan hut that belongs to the Perugia branch of CAI.

WALK

From the Sibillini Park signboard at **Forca di Presta** (1534m), path n.101 starts its long tiring ascent due N. It crosses the stony flanks of Costa le Particelle, which are anchored by domes of silver-white mouse-ear plants, views improving over the Piano Grande with each step you take. Occasional red/white markers show the way, and are best followed in preference to the multiple variants which encourage erosion. Several commemorative crosses are passed en route, including **Croce Zilioli** (1922m), just after an ample saddle with views down Valle Santa, which opens W. It's a steady ascent on a good path over 2052m **Monte Vettoretto**. Abrupt steep tracts ensue as Pratopulito is traversed to the stone hut Rifugio Zilioli (2233m) sheltering below broad elongated **Sella delle Ciaule** (2hrs, 2240m), dialect for 'crows'. Unusual long trenches mark the crest which hosts a divine spread of intense blue gentians and Apennine edelweiss, almost flush with the ground to minimise blasting by the winds. An imposing rock wall bounds the NW horizon: close at hand is Cima del Lago succeeded by Cima del Redentore and sheer Pizzo del Diavolo. The crest also overlooks a beautiful grass and rubble cirque dotted with tiny dolinas.

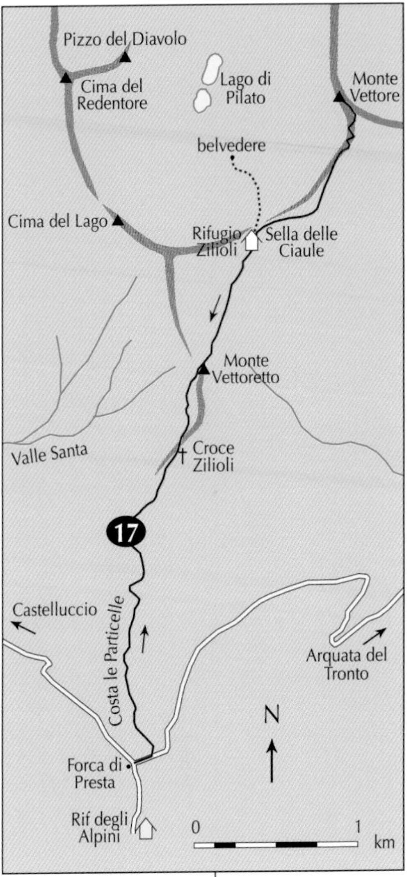

Monte Vettore summit

N.101 moves off NE for the long slog up bare slopes, concluding in zigzags at a cross, deceptive as the actual peak is slightly further up. **Monte Vettore** itself (45mins, 2476m) is brilliant, though in a high wind you'll want to keep a low profile. The Adriatic Sea stretches out E beyond the rolling Piceno hills, while Corno Grande, Gran Sasso and Monti della Laga spread out SE. A few steps along the ridge is a tempting glimpse of Lago di Pilato at the foot of dizzy Pizzo del Diavolo, backed by Monte Sibilla NNW.

Retrace your steps to **Sella delle Ciaule** (30mins, 2240m).

Extension to Lago di Pilato Belvedere (40mins return)
From the broad saddle plunge N via the grassy slopes, a veritable flowered carpet of violets and pasque flowers. Keep to the R of the minor streambed, pointing your boots in the direction of the modest rocky barrier on the edge of this sheltered cirque. This serves as a perfect **Belvedere** (2175m) over the lake. Afterwards climb back up the same way to **Sella della Ciaule** (2240m).

Lago di Pilato beneath Pizzo del Diavolo

The final leg back down to **Forca di Presta** (1534m) takes 1hr.

Forca di Presta: Rifugio degli Alpini ☎ 0736 809278, sleeps 34, open mid-June to mid-Sept + many weekends; with memorable meals and a great atmosphere.

Rifugio Zilioli – see www.caiperugia.it.

WALK 18

Monte delle Rose

Walking time	4hrs 10mins
Difficulty	Grade 2
Ascent/descent	665m/665m
Distance	13.8km/8.5 miles
Start/Finish	Castelluccio
Access	Castelluccio can be reached by road from any of three directions – Norcia, Visso and Castelsantangelo sul Nera or via Forca di Presta. The only bus comes from Norcia on Thursdays.

The opening stage of this lovely walk curves over the Piano Perduto, a medium altitude pasture basin adjoining the famous Piano Grande (see Walk 19).

Its name, 'lost plain', refers to a milestone 1522 battle between Visso and Norcia over territorial rights, though the passage of time has exaggerated the narrative a little. The numerically superior Norcians, with 6000 men, were pitted against a piddling 600 soldiers from Visso; however, the latter called in their female forces who successfully distracted the opposite side, though exactly how can only be speculated upon. The whole lot were massacred, the plain running red with blood. Nowadays colour comes from the dense concentrations of wildflowers, such as the veritable rivers of yellow mustard blooms in the fields of lentil crops, contrasting with the divine wild peonies on the edge of woodland in little-visited Valle Canatra. Pristine green – or russet in autumn – comes from the foliage of the magnificent beech trees on the mountain slopes, one of the few remaining ancient woods in the Sibillini, 1000 hectares in extent.

This rewarding loop route offers plenty of variety, vast views included. The way is fairly straightforward despite the lack of waymarking, though a compass comes in handy. Both description and map need to be followed with care, especially in low cloud and limited visibility. It makes a perfect first walk in the Sibillini as

Mustard blooms in Valle Canatra

you get an excellent overall idea of the Piano Grande and Piano Perduto, as well as the main crest with its landmark peaks such as Cima del Redentore.

A 1hr 15min extension is feasible to Monte Patino, viewpoint extraordinaire over the lovely walled Umbrian town of Norcia (see below).

WALK

From the main car park at **Castelluccio** (1452m) take the road N (in the direction of Castelsantangelo), but a short way along fork L (NW) on an unmarked gravel lane. It rounds the corner through beech copses to enter Valle Canatra with good views over to the medieval battleground on Piano Perduto. Past grazing land is a picnic area and the drinking troughs of **Fonte di Canatra** (30mins, 1360m).

A clear lane proceeds W alongside fields, while ahead rises Monte delle Rose at the end of this valley. Gradually, ever-thicker beech woods obscure the surrounding mountain flanks. At a conspicuous clearing

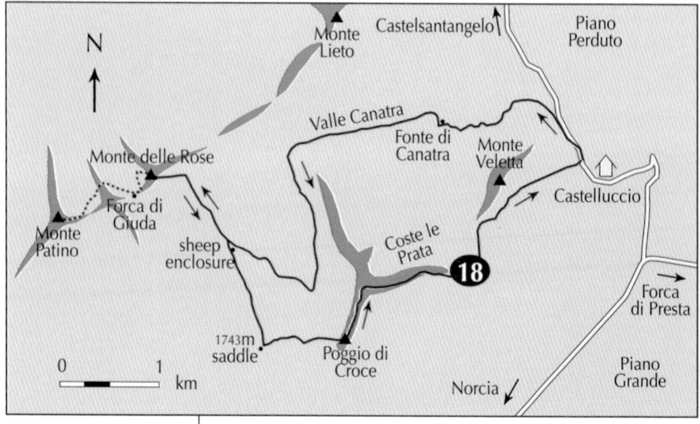

used by wood cutters (20mins, 1486m) turn L (S) uphill via a pretty, shady side valley. The route narrows to a faint path. In the upper reaches a lane is joined – turn R across open pasture and gently uphill. Beautiful clusters of ancient, gnarled beech trees are passed, then **sheep enclosures** on a broad crest with the GAS (Grande Anello). Behind you stretch the central Sibillini while ahead are Monte Patino with its cross WNW, and Monte delle Rose NW. Follow the red/white markers NW on a track until the GAS veers away L (for Forca di Giuda) – but you continue straight on. Around the 1750m mark, corresponding to the head of Valle Canatra, leave the track and cut L up the flowered slopes to the top of **Monte delle Rose** (1hr 20mins, 1861m), marked by a large cairn. ◂

Now, take in the wonderful views over the rolling hills of Umbria, clad in dark woods, while from the other side of this lookout are almost complete views of the Sibillini peaks and the linking crests.

Extension to Monte Patino

From Monte delle Rose it's a brilliant idea to drop W to **Forca di Giuda** (15mins, 1794m) then proceed on the 1hr return path to 1883m **Monte Patino** and the enjoyable view of Norcia and its intact system of defensive walls – see Walk 14.

Subsequently, from Forca di Giuda follow red/white GAS markings SSE back to the **sheep enclosures** in the main walk.

View of Castelluccio from Poggio di Croce

Afterwards make your way back down to the track and rejoin the red/white GAS. Stick carefully with the markings past the **sheep enclosures**, ignoring the lane followed on the way up. Head SSE with the GAS, across stony–grassy slopes to an unnamed **saddle** at 1743m. Leaving the GAS now, take the faint path L (E) signed for Castelluccio. You can see all the way across the Piano Grande, while in the distance SE are the snow-spattered Monti della Laga. Closer at hand due E is Poggio di Croce, your next destination, identifiable by what look like giant fingernail scratches gouged down it. At a 1742m saddle a wide, white track is crossed (NB this track leads directly to Castelluccio but it's not half as much fun or as scenic as this detour). Continue E on a faint lane, soon climbing steeply to the cairn and pole atop **Poggio di Croce** (1hr, 1833m) and great views. Then, with no path as such head NNE along the flowered ridge line to another pole on an unnamed peak at 1850m, for an even vaster outlook over the entire Piano Grande and a bird's-eye view of Castelluccio, backed by the Sibillini spine. After a short stretch NE along Coste le Prata, cut steeply downhill to the edge of beech woods and turn L onto the wide, white track crossed earlier. The final tract coasts below Monte Veletta, a popular launching point with hang-gliders. The route concludes happily back at the car park of **Castelluccio** (1hr, 1452m).

Castelluccio: Taverna di Castelluccio ☎ 0743 821158 www.tavernacastelluccio.it
Locanda de' Senari ☎ 0743 821205 www.agriturismosenari.it

Flowered fields at the foot at Castelluccio

WALK 19

Castelluccio and the Piano Grande

Walking time	4hrs + 40mins for exploring the Mergani
Difficulty	Grade 1
Ascent/descent	200m/200m
Distance	15.5km/9.6 miles
Start/Finish	Castelluccio
Access	Castelluccio can be reached by road from any of three directions – from Norcia, Visso and Castelsantangelo or via Forca di Presta. The only bus comes from Norcia on Thursdays.

Whichever way the vast altopiano is approached, the aptly named Piano Grande or Great Plain comes as quite a surprise after the rolling hills of Umbria or the Marche.

An immense flat-bottomed basin it extends approximately 18 km^2 at an altitude of 1200m above sea level. It is ringed with elongated crests which rise well over the 2400m mark on the westernmost edge, encompassing the Sibillini's highest peaks. It takes no great stretch of the imagination to picture the long-gone lake here, which drained away during the Pleistocene era, disappearing from view little by little through channels culminating in the depths of a sinkhole in the southwest corner, the Inghiottitoio (a marvellously evocative Italian word that suggests swallowing or gulping). Despite lengthy investigation, researchers have yet to discover where the water flows out, though most believe it emerges 700 metres lower down on the Piano di Santa Scolastica in the proximity of Norcia. The channnels themselves make for an educational visit. Called *mergani* from the Latin for 'subside', the 3m wide, 2m deep grassy ditches crowded with clumps of reeds also provide wildlife with a handy hiding place. Foxes lurk in there, checking the progress of oblivious crows attracted in turn by the chance of a feast on the carcasses of reckless thirsty sheep who clamber into the ditches to drink, then get stuck.

Over time, shattered rock debris and soil from the surrounding mountains have built up on the Piano Grande. Thick beech woods and even fir flourished here long ago, but these were put to the axe to make way for grazing sheep. Nowadays only patches of trees survive on the island-knolls such as Monte Guaidone on the southeastern edge. Strips of arable land are sown with tiny lentils, a variety famed all over Italy. In wintertime snow covers the fields, transforming them into a huge cross-country ski arena. In medieval times, terrible tempestuous weather led the church authorities to decree that bells be rung ceaselessly in white-out conditions to help guide travellers unfortunate enough to have been caught out in a blizzard during a crossing. They would also toll to warn villagers of impending sheep rustlers.

On the eastern edge of the Piano Grande, halfway up Cima del Redentore, is a gigantic white gash. *Strada delle fate*, the 'fairies' way' was gouged out by one of the Sibilla's handmaidens who got caught out by the arrival of dawn and had to get home in a hurry (see Walk 10 for more).

Piano Grande below Castelluccio

Poppies and mustard on the Piano Grande

The Piano Grande is spectacular at any time of year, but it attracts overwhelming floods of visitors in early June for the breathtaking, colourful spectacle of the Fiorita. Almost overnight the strips of fields assume incredible colours, broad brush strokes of watercolour. The pulse and cereal crops encourage the growth of a brilliant palette of wildflowers – vivid purple–yellow–red–crimson thanks to mustard and cornflowers, poppies and vetch. Even the uncultivated areas are a blaze of colour with campanulas, yellow gentians, scented pinks, bistort and thrift. An unforgettable spectacle and a great challenge for photographers and bees alike!

In the north of the Piano Grande a prominent conical hill hosts the curious cluttered village Castelluccio di Norcia. Legend attributes its first settlement to a colony of Jews sent packing from Rome by Emperor Vespasian. However, historical records set the date in the Middle Ages with the construction of a castle in the 13th century – Castelluccio means 'cute little castle'. With a permanent population down to 12, this wind-battered rural community has survived on its traditional activities, such as sheep herding and making *pecorino* (sheep) cheese, though these have now inevitably been supplemented by tourism. For centuries it was the stronghold of women and children for months on end as generations of menfolk tended the flocks and accompanied the livestock on the yearly transhumance. Nowadays, the village has a handful of good B&Bs, rustic restaurants and a sprinkling of stalls selling cheese and sausages. Wide-scale renewal was underway at the time of writing and new establishments will undoubtedly appear.

Especially memorable when the wildflowers are in bloom, it is also fascinating in autumn, when it is clothed in infinite shades of yellow and brown.

The highly recommended walk described here is a wonderful loop that wanders across the Piano Grande to the sinkhole. It is simple and relaxing. At a couple of places the way is unclear but in good weather visual landmarks are abundant, so progress is straightforward. Despite numbering on the commercial map there is no actual waymarking on the ground. ◂ Drinking water and sun protection are essential.

WALK

Leave **Castelluccio** (1452m) on the rough lane alongside Albergo Sibilla, to descend gently S to the plain, passing between fields. The lane keeps well away from the road, at the base of hills whose flanks are heavily scarred with centuries of spidery livestock tracks. A tiny chapel stands at the foot of a map of Italy made entirely out of conifers, planted by the Forestry Commission in the 1950s to celebrate an anniversary! The lane peters out as you approach a barbed wire fence – a rudimentary string gate lets walkers through to the water troughs of **Fontanile** (40mins, 1290m). Turn L for the road and a camper van parking area with a summer **snack bar**. Across the road is a horse-riding enclosure where you turn R on the tarmac. (Don't be tempted by the lane ESE popular with the 4WDs transporting hang-gliders to the launching pads on La Rotonda.)

Only minutes further along is a rusty shed where you need the rutted lane L (SE) traversing a vast, uncultivated and prairie-like swathe of the Piano Grande.

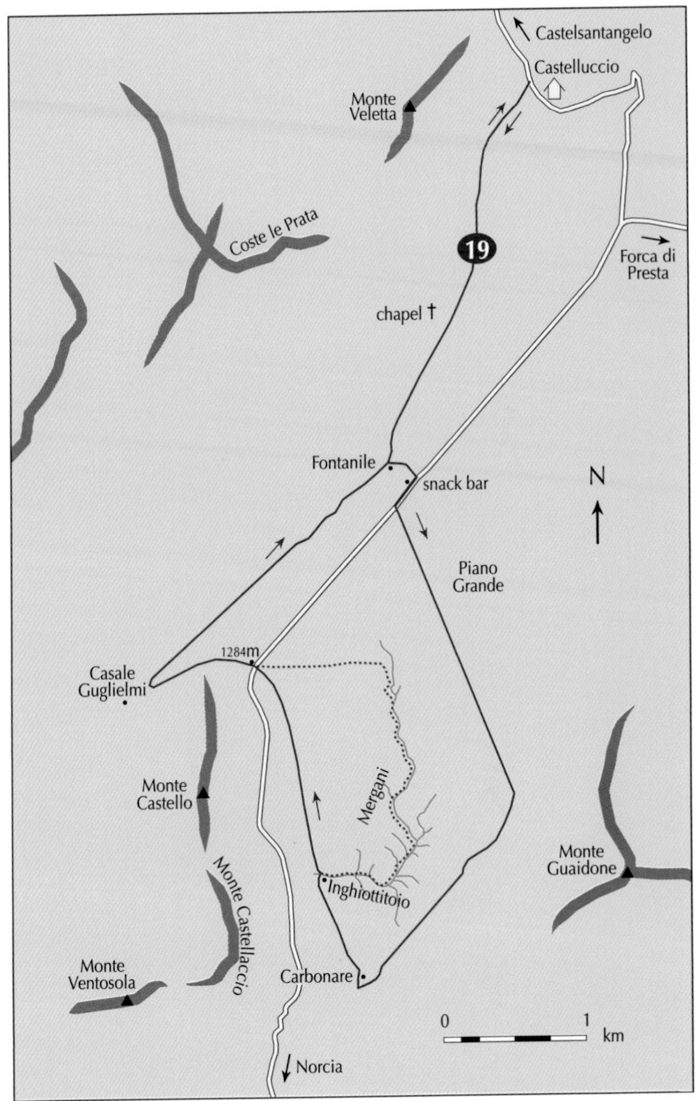
Castelsantangelo
Castelluccio
Monte Veletta
Coste le Prata
19
Forca di Presta
chapel
Fontanile
snack bar
N
Piano Grande
1284m
Casale Guglielmi
Monte Castello
Mergani
Monte Castellaccio
Inghiottitoio
Monte Guaidone
Monte Ventosola
Carbonare
0
1
km
Norcia

Castelluccio

Twittering winchats, which feed on the seeds in the knee-high grass, can be deafening on this stretch, as can crickets and bees. Now you're heading for Monte Guaidone, a helpful landmark on the landscape ahead. As the track becomes fainter, you link into a clearer one R (SW) tracing the base of the afore-mentioned mount. This leads over a slight rise before disappearing. Fear not, but continue SW following a low embankment and head for the stone hut **Carbonare** (1272m), a reference to the charcoal burners of the past.

Now it's NNW as far as the power line, where a faint path takes you into a depression for the opening of the **Inghiottitoio** (1hr 30mins, 1257m) at the foot of an outcrop beneath Monte Castellaccio. While not that impressive to actually see, as the opening is covered with wire netting, it is of key significance for the Piano Grande.

Exploring the Mergani (40mins)
It's definitely worthwhile turning E to venture along the Mergani ditches, though interest will depend on the time of year and water flow. Keeping a vigilant eye out for marshy patches, follow the sheep paths parallel to the channel floor. By keeping L at each ramification it is possible to emerge on the plain and cut across L (W) to the **1284m** point on the road.

Up the other side of the depression you touch on a series of semi-circular dolinas, the result of karstification. A clear lane is joined and leads N amidst tiny gentians and pretty narcissus to the **road at 1284m** (20mins).

A track used by shepherds heads W into a side valley at the foot of Monte Castello. This leads to drinking troughs at the ruined huts **Casale Guglielmi** (1309m, used as the location for Zeffirelli's film about the life of Saint Francis of Assisi). However, a tad before the structure turn R (NE) on the faint lane at the foot of a series of terraced slopes and proceed as far as the **Fontanile** (45mins, 1284m) encountered earlier on. Return to **Castelluccio** (45mins, 1452m).

The Mergani

Castelluccio: Taverna di Castelluccio ☎ 0743 821158 www.taverna castelluccio.it
Locanda de' Senari ☎ 0743 821205 www.agriturismosenari.it

WALK 20

The Dogana Loop

Walking time	4hrs
Difficulty	Grade 1–2
Ascent/descent	430m/430m
Distance	15.5km/9.6 miles
Start/Finish	Forca di Presta
Access	Road pass Forca di Presta is a short drive from Castelluccio, or a slightly longer one from either Norcia or Arquata del Tronto.

A stunningly rewarding circuit in the southeastern corner of the renowned Piano Grande, this takes in the pretty Dogana and Piano Piccolo offshoots, little known to walkers.

The outward stretch uses a fragment of the long-distance GAS (Grande Anello dei Sibillini) via a succession of scenic ridges, with far-reaching views to the Monti della Laga, which extend over neighbouring Lazio and Abruzzo. And the memorable vistas over the vast Piano Grande are not to be glossed over, an inspiring spectacle at any time of year. Halfway along the walk, at Colle Le Cese is a decent *rifugio* and restaurant should any refreshments be needed.

The place name Forca di Presta, where the route begins, is believed to derive from either *prestito* for 'loan', referring to ancient land leasing practices, or possibly from *praesto* for 'a place high up'. Dogana on the other hand means 'customs', in this case denoting a valley close to the old border between the Kingdom of Naples and the Papal States.

WALK

From **Forca di Presta** (1534m) set out along the lane due S, signed for the GAS. With fleeting views over the vast expanse of Piano Grande, only a short walk away is friendly, old-style **Rifugio degli Alpini** at 1574m. Continue in slight ascent on the broad gravel track, across bare pastureland skirting Monte Pellicciara. Not

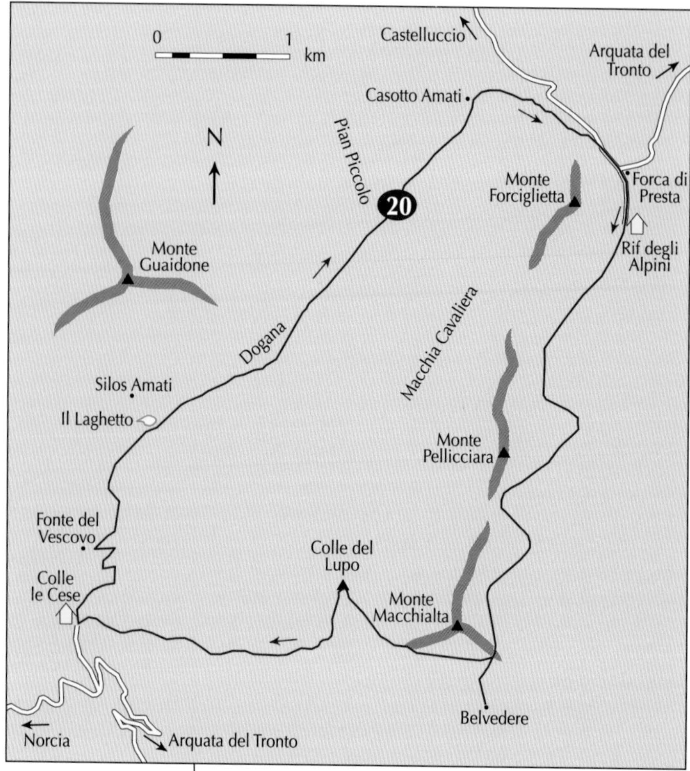

far on, where the track bears W, take the short detour L along a wooden walkway to a **Belvedere** where helpful photo panels identify mountain ranges near and far. For instance, standing out dramatically to the SE is Pizzo del Selva in the Monti della Laga range, while in the distant E is the light-coloured massif Monte dei Fiori.

Back at the start of the walkway proceed due W on the wide track beneath Monte Macchialta. Where a corner is rounded watch out for the faintly marked path R (NW) uphill over karstic terrain. A modest rise is reached with stunning views over the Piano Grande

Hang glider in Pian Piccolo

altopiano and hilltop Castelluccio, not to mention the central Sibillini peaks. At **Colle del Lupo** (1610m, col of the wolf) turn L (SSW) onto a lane back into beech woods, soon to become broad scenic crests. Then it's W to the broad saddle and low key ski area of **Colle le Cese** (2hrs, 1484m).

Close to Rifugio di Colle le Cese, a clear lane with red/white marking for n.557 goes N through beech woods, descending in curves to the broad pasture valley known as Dogana. At the **Fonte del Vescovo** (bishop's spring) drinking troughs it bears NE in the shade of the gentle slopes of Monte Guaidone. Not far along is the curious Silos Amati (the Amati family were important landowners here) near creatively named **Il Laghetto** (little lake) at 1370m, with rushes, water fowl and frogs galore. Now an orange earth track leads along the broad trough of Dogana, at the far end of which rises the unmistakable Redentore–Vettore massif. Alongside E the mountain flanks are largely carpeted by the so-called Macchia Cavaliera beech woods, a mere fragment of the ancient

Striding out in the Dogana valley

forest that once covered the entire Piano Grande and surrounds. The bare ridge above it is a favourite launching pad for hang gliders. About 1hr from Colle Le Cese, as the valley and the track bear L into Piano Piccolo, take care not to miss the fainter lane R (red/white marker in the middle of the track), still NE. Accompanied by skylarks and swallows and pretty thrift flowers, the way proceeds to ruined **Casotto Amati** (1373m). Soon afterwards leave the lane for a path R (E) uphill below the road at the foot of Monte Vettoretto. The tarmac is joined very briefly as you climb past a spring spouting deliciously cool water, to arrive at **Forca di Presta** (2hrs, 1534m), and the walk's end.

Forca di Presta: Rifugio degli Alpini (☎ 0736 809278 www.rifugiomontisibillini.it), sleeps 34, open mid-June to mid-Sept + many weekends; with memorable meals and a great atmosphere.

Colle le Cese: Rifugio di Colle le Cese (☎ 0736 808102 www.rifugiocollelecese.it), sleeps 37. A hotel rather than a walkers' refuge, this place offers comfortable rooms with en suites.

WALK 21

I Pantani

Walking time	1hr 45mins
Difficulty	Grade 1
Ascent/descent	190m/190m
Distance	7.3km/4.5 miles
Start/Finish	Forca Canapine
Access	The road pass Forca Canapine can be reached from either Norcia or Arquata del Tronto.

At the Pantani marshes soil and clay have accumulated on a limestone base, creating an attractive fertile basin where surface water lies in shallow lakes. Strange as it may seem, in the hot summer months these have been known to change colour, assuming a bright crimson

Rifugio Ratti at Forca Canapine

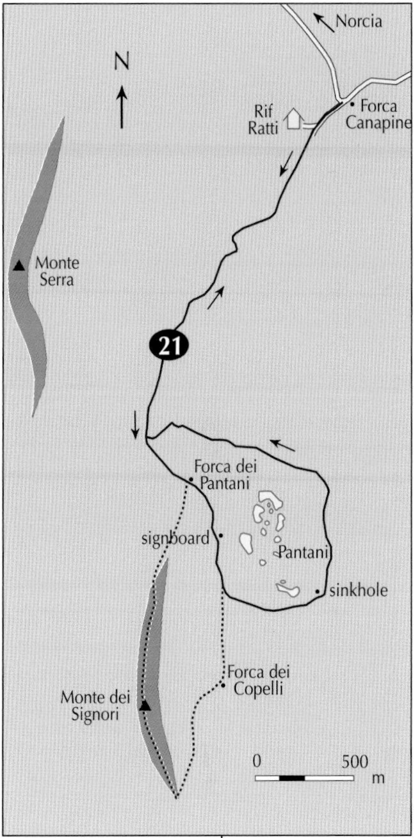

sheen due to the action of a microscopic alga which spreads through the water when the temperature is between 15 and 19°C. Masses of gorgeous wildflowers add to the allure. Just out of the extreme southerly edge of the Sibillini park, this is an agreeable stroll on wide tracks, easily recognisable thanks to regular red/white markings. All around are rolling hills and knolls, given over to both beech woods and rich pasture that is enjoyed by grazing livestock. The Pantani are a popular family picnic spot on summer weekends. A variant of similar length is given via the elongated ridge of Monte dei Signori, 'mount of the lords', the former boundary between the Kingdom of Naples and the Papal States. However, any number of variations are feasible by wandering across the neighbouring hills.

Family-run Rifugio Ratti at the walk start makes a handy base.

WALK

From the road pass **Forca Canapine** (1541m) take the white rock-based lane marked SI (for long-distance Sentiero Italia). Passing above Rifugio Ratti it heads SW, coasting along the upper tree line with lovely views to the snow-spattered Monti della Laga SE. Vast rolling landscapes open out. Modest Monte Serra is soon

Cyclist at I Pantani

passed with its ski lifts, and you swing gradually up to minor saddle **Forca dei Pantani** (1607m), at the foot of the elongated crest of Monte dei Signori. This is the entry to the basin housing the scatter of Pantani lakes. A short distance downhill a **signboard** (30mins) for the SI is passed and you continue S to a fork for a 4WD track that branches L (W).

Variant via Monte dei Signori (40mins)

From the fork after the **signboard** continue S to the saddle **Forca dei Copelli** (1626m) then branch diagonally R on the fainter lane through beech woods. This emerges at a 1702m saddle and from there you make your way up the grassy slopes to the 1781m top of **Monte dei Signori**. From there it's due N in gentle descent to Forca dei Pantani.

In the basin's SE corner is an interesting **sinkhole** at 1596m. Above it, turn L to leave the track and follow the modest up-and-down ridge N, enjoying the great outlook NE to the landmark Redentore-Vettore massif. To continue circling above the lakes, towards the NE corner, take the faint track NW in gentle ascent to the crest and an old stone marker dating back to 1847, shortly prior to the Unification of Italy. Now it stands on the three-way border between the regions of Lazio, Marche and Umbria. Not far downhill rejoin the lane taken on the outward leg of the circuit, a short distance from Forca dei Pantani. Turn R (N) for the 30min return to **Forca Canapine** (1541m).

Rifugio Genziana, formerly known as Rifugio Vittorio Ratti
☎ 0743 828623, sleeps 20, open June–Oct

APPENDIX

Italian–English Glossary

abbazia	abbey
acqua (non) potabile	(un)drinkable water
affittacamere	B&B
agriturismo	farm stay
aiuto!	help!
albergo	hotel
alto	high
anello	ring
autobus	bus
autostazione	bus station
borgo	village, small town
caduta sassi	rockfalls
camere libere	rooms available
campo	field
capanna, casale, casotto	hut
casa	house
cascata	waterfall
castello	castle
chiesa	church
cima	mountain peak
cimitero	cemetery
colle	hill
croce	cross
diga	dam
est/orientale	east/eastern
facile	easy
fermata	bus stop
ferrovia	railway
fiume	river
fonte, fontanile	spring (water)
forca	col, pass
forra	ravine
fosso	lit. ditch, but used for valley and watercourse
frazione	hamlet
gola	gorge, canyon
grotta	cave

incrocio	crossroads, intersection
lago	lake
maneggio	horse-riding
mulattiera	mule track
municipio	local council
nord/settentrionale	north/northern
orario	timetable
ovest/occidentale	west/western
pantano	bog
parcheggio	car park
passeggiata	promenade, walk
passarella pedonale	footbridge
pedonale	for pedestrians
percorso	route
pericolo/pericoloso	danger/dangerous
piano	plain, plateau (noun) or slowly, quietly (adv)
piazza	town square
pizzo	mountain peak, point
poggio	modest mountain, hilltop
ponte	bridge
prato	meadow, field
Pro Loco	local tourist office
pullman	bus
punta	point, mountain peak
rifugio	mountain hut or inn, usually manned
rocca	castle
sede	headquarters
sella	saddle, col
sentiero	walking path
soccorso alpino	mountain rescue
sorgente	spring (water)
stazione ferroviaria	railway station
sterrata	dirt road
stretta	narrow valley
sud/meridionale	south/southern
tornante	hairpin bend
torre	tower
torrente	mountain stream
val, valle, vallon, vallone	valley

NOTES

NOTES

LISTING OF CICERONE GUIDES

BRITISH ISLES CHALLENGES, COLLECTIONS AND ACTIVITIES

The End to End Trail
The Mountains of England and Wales
1 Wales & 2 England
The National Trails
The Relative Hills of Britain
The Ridges of England, Wales and Ireland
The UK Trailwalker's Handbook
The UK's County Tops
Three Peaks, Ten Tors

MOUNTAIN LITERATURE

Unjustifiable Risk?

UK CYCLING

Border Country Cycle Routes
Cycling in the Hebrides
Cycling in the Peak District
Cycling the Pennine Bridleway
Mountain Biking in the Lake District
Mountain Biking in the Yorkshire Dales
Mountain Biking on the South Downs
The C2C Cycle Route
The End to End Cycle Route
The Lancashire Cycleway

SCOTLAND

Backpacker's Britain
Central and Southern Scottish Highlands
Northern Scotland
Ben Nevis and Glen Coe
Great Mountain Days in Scotland
North to the Cape
Not the West Highland Way
Scotland's Best Small Mountains
Scotland's Far West
Scotland's Mountain Ridges
Scrambles in Lochaber
The Ayrshire and Arran Coastal Paths
The Border Country
The Cape Wrath Trail
The Great Glen Way
The Isle of Mull
The Isle of Skye
The Pentland Hills
The Southern Upland Way
The Speyside Way
The West Highland Way
Walking Highland Perthshire
Walking in Scotland's Far North
Walking in the Angus Glens
Walking in the Cairngorms
Walking in the Ochils, Campsie Fells and Lomond Hills
Walking in Torridon
Walking Loch Lomond and the Trossachs
Walking on Harris and Lewis
Walking on Jura, Islay and Colonsay
Walking on Rum and the Small Isles
Walking on the Isle of Arran
Walking on the Orkney and Shetland Isles
Walking on Uist and Barra
Walking the Corbetts
1 South of the Great Glen
2 North of the Great Glen
Walking the Galloway Hills
Walking the Lowther Hills
Walking the Munros
1 Southern, Central and Western Highlands
2 Northern Highlands and the Cairngorms
Winter Climbs Ben Nevis and Glen Coe
Winter Climbs in the Cairngorms
World Mountain Ranges: Scotland

NORTHERN ENGLAND TRAILS

A Northern Coast to Coast Walk
Backpacker's Britain
Northern England
Hadrian's Wall Path
The Dales Way
The Pennine Way
The Spirit of Hadrian's Wall

NORTH EAST ENGLAND, YORKSHIRE DALES AND PENNINES

Great Mountain Days in the Pennines
Historic Walks in North Yorkshire
South Pennine Walks
St Oswald's Way and St Cuthbert's Way
The Cleveland Way and the Yorkshire Wolds Way
The North York Moors
The Reivers Way
The Teesdale Way
The Yorkshire Dales
North and East
South and West
Walking in County Durham
Walking in Northumberland
Walking in the North Pennines
Walks in Dales Country
Walks in the Yorkshire Dales
Walks on the North York Moors – Books 1 & 2

NORTH WEST ENGLAND AND THE ISLE OF MAN

Historic Walks in Cheshire
Isle of Man Coastal Path
The Isle of Man
The Lune Valley and Howgills
The Ribble Way
Walking in Cumbria's Eden Valley
Walking in Lancashire
Walking in the Forest of Bowland and Pendle
Walking on the West Pennine Moors
Walks in Lancashire Witch Country
Walks in Ribble Country
Walks in Silverdale and Arnside
Walks in the Forest of Bowland

LAKE DISTRICT

Coniston Copper Mines
Great Mountain Days in the Lake District
Lake District Winter Climbs
Lakeland Fellranger
The Central Fells
The Far-Eastern Fells
The Mid-Western Fells
The Near Eastern Fells
The Northern Fells
The North-Western Fells
The Southern Fells
The Western Fells
Roads and Tracks of the Lake District

Rocky Rambler's Wild Walks
Scrambles in the Lake District
North & South
Short Walks in Lakeland
1 South Lakeland
2 North Lakeland
3 West Lakeland
The Cumbria Coastal Way
The Cumbria Way and the
Allerdale Ramble
Tour of the Lake District

DERBYSHIRE, PEAK DISTRICT AND MIDLANDS

High Peak Walks
Scrambles in the Dark Peak
The Star Family Walks
Walking in Derbyshire
White Peak Walks
The Northern Dales
The Southern Dales

SOUTHERN ENGLAND

A Walker's Guide to the
Isle of Wight
Suffolk Coast & Heaths Walks
The Cotswold Way
The North Downs Way
The Peddars Way and Norfolk
Coast Path
The Ridgeway National Trail
The South Downs Way
The South West Coast Path
The Thames Path
Walking in Berkshire
Walking in Kent
Walking in Sussex
Walking in the Isles of Scilly
Walking in the New Forest
Walking in the Thames Valley
Walking on Dartmoor
Walking on Guernsey
Walking on Jersey
Walking on the Isle of Wight
Walks in the South Downs
National Park

WALES AND WELSH BORDERS

Backpacker's Britain – Wales
Glyndwr's Way
Great Mountain Days in
Snowdonia
Hillwalking in Snowdonia
Hillwalking in Wales
Vols 1 & 2
Offa's Dyke Path
Ridges of Snowdonia
Scrambles in Snowdonia
The Ascent of Snowdon
Lleyn Peninsula Coastal Path
Pembrokeshire Coastal Path
The Shropshire Hills
The Wye Valley Walk
Walking in Pembrokeshire
Walking in the
Forest of Dean
Walking in the South
Wales Valleys
Walking on Gower
Walking on the Brecon Beacons
Welsh Winter Climbs

INTERNATIONAL CHALLENGES, COLLECTIONS AND ACTIVITIES

Canyoning
Europe's High Points
The Via Francigena
(Canterbury to Rome): Part 1

EUROPEAN CYCLING

Cycle Touring in France
Cycle Touring in Ireland
Cycle Touring in Spain
Cycle Touring in Switzerland
Cycling in the French Alps
Cycling the Canal du Midi
Cycling the River Loire
The Danube Cycleway
The Grand Traverse of the
Massif Central
The Rhine Cycle Route
The Way of St James

AFRICA

Climbing in the Moroccan
Anti-Atlas
Kilimanjaro
Mountaineering in the
Moroccan High Atlas
The High Atlas
Trekking in the Atlas Mountains
Walking in the Drakensberg

ALPS – CROSS-BORDER ROUTES

100 Hut Walks in the Alps
Across the Eastern Alps: E5
Alpine Points of View
Alpine Ski Mountaineering
1 Western Alps
2 Central and Eastern Alps
Chamonix to Zermatt
Snowshoeing
Tour of Mont Blanc
Tour of Monte Rosa
Tour of the Matterhorn
Trekking in the Alps
Walking in the Alps
Walks and Treks in the
Maritime Alps

PYRENEES AND FRANCE/ SPAIN CROSS-BORDER ROUTES

Rock Climbs in The Pyrenees
The GR10 Trail
The Mountains of Andorra
The Pyrenean Haute Route
The Pyrenees
The Way of St James
France & Spain
Through the Spanish Pyrenees:
GR11
Walks and Climbs in
the Pyrenees

AUSTRIA

The Adlerweg
Trekking in Austria's
Hohe Tauern
Trekking in the Stubai Alps
Trekking in the Zillertal Alps
Walking in Austria

EASTERN EUROPE

The High Tatras
The Mountains of Romania
Walking in Bulgaria's
National Parks
Walking in Hungary

FRANCE

Chamonix Mountain Adventures
Ecrins National Park
GR20: Corsica
Mont Blanc Walks
Mountain Adventures in
the Maurienne
The Cathar Way
The GR5 Trail
The Robert Louis Stevenson Trail
Tour of the Oisans: The GR54

Tour of the Queyras
Tour of the Vanoise
Trekking in the Vosges and Jura
Vanoise Ski Touring
Walking in the Auvergne
Walking in the Cathar Region
Walking in the Cevennes
Walking in the Dordogne
Walking in the Haute Savoie North & South
Walking in the Languedoc
Walking in the Tarentaise and Beaufortain Alps
Walking on Corsica

GERMANY

Germany's Romantic Road
Walking in the Bavarian Alps
Walking in the Harz Mountains
Walking the River Rhine Trail

HIMALAYA

Annapurna
Bhutan: A Trekker's Guide
Everest: A Trekker's Guide
Garhwal and Kumaon: A Trekker's and Visitor's Guide
Kangchenjunga: A Trekker's Guide
Langtang with Gosainkund and Helambu: A Trekker's Guide
Manaslu: A Trekker's Guide
The Mount Kailash Trek
Trekking in Ladakh

ICELAND & GREENLAND

Trekking in Greenland
Walking and Trekking in Iceland

IRELAND

Irish Coastal Walks
The Irish Coast to Coast Walk
The Mountains of Ireland

ITALY

Gran Paradiso
Sibillini National Park
Stelvio National Park
Shorter Walks in the Dolomites
Through the Italian Alps
Trekking in the Apennines
Trekking in the Dolomites
Via Ferratas of the Italian Dolomites: Vols 1 & 2
Walking in Abruzzo
Walking in Sardinia
Walking in Sicily
Walking in the Central Italian Alps
Walking in the Dolomites
Walking in Tuscany
Walking on the Amalfi Coast
Walking the Italian Lakes

MEDITERRANEAN

Jordan – Walks, Treks, Caves, Climbs and Canyons
The Ala Dag
The High Mountains of Crete
The Mountains of Greece
Treks and Climbs in Wadi Rum, Jordan
Walking in Malta
Western Crete

NORTH AMERICA

British Columbia
The Grand Canyon
The John Muir Trail
The Pacific Crest Trail

SOUTH AMERICA

Aconcagua and the Southern Andes
Hiking and Biking Peru's Inca Trails
Torres del Paine

SCANDINAVIA

Walking in Norway

SLOVENIA, CROATIA AND MONTENEGRO

The Julian Alps of Slovenia
The Mountains of Montenegro
Trekking in Slovenia
Walking in Croatia
Walking in Slovenia: The Karavanke

SPAIN AND PORTUGAL

Costa Blanca: West
Mountain Walking in Southern Catalunya
The Mountains of Central Spain
The Northern Caminos
Trekking through Mallorca
Walking in Madeira
Walking in Mallorca
Walking in the Algarve
Walking in the Cordillera Cantabrica
Walking in the Sierra Nevada
Walking on La Gomera and El Hierro
Walking on La Palma
Walking on Tenerife
Walking the GR7 in Andalucia
Walks and Climbs in the Picos de Europa

SWITZERLAND

Alpine Pass Route
Canyoning in the Alps
Central Switzerland
The Bernese Alps
The Swiss Alps
Tour of the Jungfrau Region
Walking in the Valais
Walking in Ticino
Walks in the Engadine

TECHNIQUES

Geocaching in the UK
Indoor Climbing
Lightweight Camping
Map and Compass
Mountain Weather
Outdoor Photography
Polar Exploration
Rock Climbing
Sport Climbing
The Book of the Bivvy
The Hillwalker's Guide to Mountaineering
The Hillwalker's Manual

MINI GUIDES

Avalanche!
Navigating with a GPS
Navigation
Pocket First Aid and Wilderness Medicine
Snow

For full information on all our guides, and to order books and eBooks, visit our website: **www.cicerone.co.uk**.

Walking – Trekking – Mountaineering – Climbing – Cycling

Over 40 years, Cicerone have built up an outstanding collection of 300 guides, inspiring all sorts of amazing adventures.

Every guide comes from extensive exploration and research by our expert authors, all with a passion for their subjects. They are frequently praised, endorsed and used by clubs, instructors and outdoor organisations.

All our titles can now be bought as **e-books** and many as iPad and Kindle files and we will continue to make all our guides available for these and many other devices.

Our website shows any **new information** we've received since a book was published. Please do let us know if you find anything has changed, so that we can pass on the latest details. On our **website** you'll also find some great ideas and lots of information, including sample chapters, contents lists, reviews, articles and a photo gallery.

It's easy to keep in touch with what's going on at Cicerone, by getting our monthly **free e-newsletter**, which is full of offers, competitions, up-to-date information and topical articles. You can subscribe on our home page and also follow us on **Facebook** and **Twitter**, as well as our **blog**.

Cicerone – the very best guides for exploring the world.

CICERONE

2 Police Square Milnthorpe Cumbria LA7 7PY

Tel: 015395 62069 info@cicerone.co.uk

www.cicerone.co.uk